中国人民大学对外语言文化学院
美国哈佛大学东亚语文系现代汉语部
合编教材

汉语基础

【第二册】

主　编：胡明扬

编写人员：岑玉珍　陈满华　黄南松　张卫国

普通话审订：张卫国

主　编：何宝璋

编写人员：陈珮嘉　胡文泽　李爱民　邱妙津

英文翻译：贾志杰

英文审订：Nick Smith

中国人民大学出版社

哈 佛 大 学　现代汉语教学部
　　　　　　　　　　　　　　　教材编写合作协议
中国人民大学对外语言文化学院

　　哈佛大学现代汉语教学部与中国人民大学对外语言文化学院本着平等互利的原则，经友好协商，决定合作编写供外国人学习汉语用的汉语教材，就编写教材有关事宜达成如下协议：

　　一、合作编写的教材首先为两个单位自身教学服务的基础教材（含音像教材和网络辅助教材），在此基础上继续合编后续教材；在满足两校使用的同时，向对外汉语教学界介绍、宣传和逐步推广。

　　二、教材编写采取主编负责制，哈佛大学方面主编为何宝璋先生，中国人民大学方面，主编为胡明扬先生。主编下可设编委会，或由编写人员和语音审订人员组成。双方主编协同负责制定编写计划、组织编写、审稿、组织出版等事宜。

　　三、为了保证教材编写工作顺利进行和完成，双方各自向有关部门提交编写教材所需的经费预算申请，争取资助。

　　四、时间：1999 年 8 月出版基础教材第一册的文字部分（课文、生词本、练习册）的试用版。

　　五、关于署名：教材出版时合作双方在封面上并列署名。在美国的用书哈佛大学现代汉语教学部署名在前，在中国的用书中国人民大学对外语言文化学院署名在前。署名者还应包括主编、每个编写人员和审订人员姓名。署名按姓氏笔画排序。

六、出版所获稿酬按照平等原则分配，在两地分别出版的稿酬，以实际工作成果为依据进行合理分配，此教材的著作权归哈佛大学现代汉语教学部与中国人民大学对外语言文化学院双方共有。

七、本协议自双方负责人签字之日起生效。有效期为 3 年，双方如无异议，到期自动延长；在合作中出现问题，双方通过平等协商解决。如终止协议，需提前 6 个月书面通知对方。

八、本协议一式四份，用汉语写成，双方各保存两份，每份具有同等效力。

哈佛大学现代汉语教学部　　中国人民大学对外语言文化学院

主任：何宝璋　　院长：郭先珍

1998 年 5 月 29 日

序

　　胡明扬教授和哈佛大学何宝璋先生联合主编的《汉语基础》教材，经过七年多的艰苦工作，终于面世了。胡明扬教授自始至终指导了教材的编写工作。

　　在中国人民大学对外语言文化学院的成立初期，我担任首任院长时，我院与哈佛大学现代汉语部于1998年夏签订了合作编写教材的协议，并请胡明扬教授和何宝璋先生担任主编。胡先生和何先生又聘请了两校优秀教师合作，排除了种种阻力和困难，对每个环节严格把关，善始善终地完成了全部编写工作。可以说这本教材是著名专家领衔主编的教材，是在科学研究基础之上编写的教材，是中美大学强强合作的成果。

　　正因为如此，这本教材具有以下几个特点：

　　教材体现了"因材施教"的原则，是以英语为代表的印欧语系零起点学生为对象的教材。教材内容考虑到学生来华学习和生活实用之必须，语法重点、难点及练习诸方面，尽量针对因中英语言及文化差异而形成的障碍来设置，并尽量贴近或适应英语语法体系及其表述方式。

　　该教材充分体现了对外汉语教学的目的性——培养学生的汉语听说能力。为此，尽量避免了以往某些教材注重词汇语法结构等知识传授而忽略语言运用的弊病，而是以培养能力为中心、以传授用法为重点。例如，对"二"和"两"、"没有"和"不"等词的用法加以区别，同时围绕用法安排了大量练习。

　　该教材针对学生学习汉语时由于中西文化差异形成的价值观念、思维方式、风俗习惯等文化障碍，编写了注释；针对学生畏惧写汉字的心理特点，专门编写了汉字笔顺表，直观而便于模仿练习，有利于学生汉字书写基本功的训练。

　　该教材充分体现了胡明扬教授一贯的学术创新和科学严谨的学风，也体现了中国人民大学和哈佛大学两校的优良治学传统。它不是以往教材的低层次重复，也不是追求功利的急就篇。教材初稿完成后，在哈佛现代汉语部试用了两遍，通过教学实践的检验，发现问题，反复修改完善，力求精益求精，力求名校教材的精品性特征。

　　这本教材，是贯彻1997年国家汉办长沙教材编写工作会议精神的成果之一。在那次会议上汉办领导组织专家对改革开放以来编写的数百种教材进行了调研，肯定了北京语言学院、北京大学等院校出版的一批优秀教材。但是也发现了两个问题：其一是教材数量虽多，质量却不够高，低水平重复多，相互模仿多，精品教材寥若晨星；其二是与国外汉语教学名校合作编写教材少，打入国际汉语教材市场有竞争力的教材也屈指可数。胡明扬教授既是为了解决长沙会议提出的问题，又融会了他和两校教师潜心科研的成果，开汉语名家编写对外汉语教材之先河。这对于对外汉语教学这个新兴学科的建设，是非常有意义的。

　　参加这本教材编写的，有中国人民大学对外语言文化学院教师岑玉珍、陈满华、黄南松、张卫国，以及哈佛大学现代汉语部教师陈珮嘉、胡文泽、李爱民、邱妙津，汉语普通话审定为中国人民大学张卫国教授，英语审定为哈佛大学 Nick Smith 先生，英文翻译为贾志杰先生。中文版教材全稿由张卫国统改一遍，胡明扬教授最后审改定稿。

　　这里，要对国家汉办表示特别的感谢。国家汉办为本教材的编写立项，并给以支持和资助，使得这本教材最终完成并顺利出版。

金　戈

2005 年

前　　言

一、编写背景

《汉语基础》是为美国大学零起点的学生编写的一套一年级汉语教材。几年前，哈佛大学因需要而准备编写一套新的既能体现当今语言事实，也能反映当前外语教学理论；既有实用性，又富于趣味性，反映大学生实际生活的初级汉语课本。中国国内经过多年对外汉语教学的实践，逐步认识到编纂国别汉语教材的重要性和必要性。在这样的情况下，美国哈佛大学东亚系现代汉语教学部和中国人民大学对外语言文化学院合作编写了这套《汉语基础》。

二、编写思路

中美合编教材首先要保证教材能在美国使用，在编写过程中要考虑美国学生学习汉语的特殊性。这个特殊性表现在课文涉及的内容和表达法在学生生活中的实用性、汉语与英语在语言结构和认知概念方面的异同，以及教学形式、课程安排等各方面。

我们考虑的是一部初级汉语教材要达到什么样的教学目的，然后根据这一目的确定以什么样的外语教学理论来指导我们的编写工作，使其在教材本身和实际课堂教学得到反映和表现以取得预期教学效果。

初级汉语教材的基本教学目的在于为学生中、高级后续学习做铺垫工作，为其今后的学习深造打下良好的基础。基于语言交际的最终目标和启发学生学习兴趣的考虑，我们认为在初级教材中应以听说入手，以学生生活最直接的环境为话语背景，从单句交际开始，逐渐深入接触话语片段，由浅及深，并在教材的后半部为后续中级教材向简单书面语过渡做前期准备。作为基础阶段的教材，《汉语基础》以语言结构为主线，涵盖了现代汉语口语中常见主要大语法现象。同时本教材以培养学生的语言交际能力为重点，涉及了广泛的话语交际情景。

三、编写指导理论

近年来，海外各种外语教学理论层出不穷，然而，"新"并不能作为教材编写的指导参数，关键要看其是否符合对外汉语教学的规律和具体教学环境的实际。对于所有的理论都不可盲目照搬，必须经过一定的研究取舍，加上一线教师亲身的教学实践总结和扬弃。我们首先在以下几个方面达成了共识：

1. 语法教学的重要性。关于语法，在对外汉语教学界普遍存在一种误解，认为那是一种人为创造出的可有可无的"规定"；或者自动联想到印欧语言曲折变化所标记的形式与意义间的联系，从而得出汉语无语法的错误概念。所谓语法，其实就是语言自身的规律，是母语说话人在语言交际过程中遵循的结构规则，这一点早已是现代语言学几代人研究的共识。

在对外汉语教学中，语法教学本身是大学外语教学的一个重要组成部分。教学理论和方法可以不同，但语法教学不能轻视，更不能放弃。研究证明，具体的语法教学有益于学生表达的准确性，也有益于学生汉语水平的提高。

2. 功能教学法，虽有很多优点，但亦有很多不足之处，可以借鉴，但不能照搬。

3. 完成"交际任务"是学生学习汉语、掌握汉语的一个重要环节。学生学习语言的目的是为了进行交际。用所学的语言交际不可能等到都学会了以后才开始。在学习过程中学生之间的互动，对学生理解和掌握所学的语法点和语言的使用是有正面作用的。所以使用或"试用"应是学习的一部分。

综上所述，我们希望本书所反映的是一种"以结构为基础的交际任务"教学。

"以结构为基础的交际任务"教学可分为如下三段式：

1. 明确每一教学单元的语法重点并配合相应练习，使学生充分理解。

2. 针对本课所学的语法点而设计多样的课堂活动和语言交际任务。初级阶段开始的教学应包括大量的模仿和机械练习，逐渐增加教具、图表等教师控制下有实际意义的课堂活动，进而过渡到学生独立完成某些交际任务。这一部分练习的特点是每一个练习都具有针对性，是为了帮助学生掌握运用某一语法点而设计的。

3. 综合交际任务。在前两阶段的基础上，教师设计一些综合交际任务的活动。这些活动的主要目的是让学生综合使用本课所学的几个语法点和重点词汇，以达到巩固和提高的目的。

四、编写原则

美国大学一般采取学期制（semester）或学季制（quarter）。平均每学年三十周。初级阶段汉语一般是每周五个学时，每天一节课。汉语作为一门选修课，由于课时有限，一般语言课听说读写几项语言技能都要包括，不可能单独开课。由于这些因素，我们的这套教材的编写原则是这样的：

1. 在一学年内可以完成《汉语基础》的全部课程。

在语言内容方面，从意义和实用功能入手，强调语言的实用性，以期达到立竿见影的效果。以美国大学生在中国学习汉语为背景，学后容易使用。课文涉及中国文化和中美异同的对比，让学生在学习语言的同时，了解中国文化，在使用时不但追求语言形式的正确，同时强调语言使用的得体、恰当。课文尽量有意思、有趣味，使学生不把学习当成包袱，当做负担。

在语法系统方面，涵括现代汉语的主要语法点，为继续学习的学生打下一个坚实的基础。不马上继续学习的学生对汉语的语法系统也能够有一个全貌的了解。

《汉语基础》兼顾听说读写四项语言技能。由于公共课的性质和课时限制，初级教材必须兼顾听说读写几个方面。除了课文和练习外，每课都有课外听力练习和阅读练习。

每一课的基本布局为：

课文部分包括课文、课文英文翻译、课文拼音注音、生词表、语法注释。

练习部分包括听力、语法、词汇、翻译和阅读等。

2. 在选题方面以美国学生在中国的生活为背景。

内容主要包括日常生活和学校生活两个方面。在日常生活方面，学生初到中国需要吃饭、问路、坐车、买东西等等。在学生的校园生活方面包括选课、爱好、专业等等。这些主题，学习时容易模拟操练，便于上口；学生学了以后，容易使用，在使用中加强理解，巩固所学内容。另外，以美国学生在中国生活为背景的好处是学生在学习语言的同时，可以了解中国的现状，了解中国和美国在生活方式、人文环境等方面的不同。

3. 语法点的选择和解释。

考虑到美国学生学习汉语的特点，英语和汉语在语法方面的异同，我们的原则是语法解释以少为宜。"少"既表现在语法点的选择上，也反映在语法点的解释上。

遇到与英语相同和近似的现象尽量不讲。以"连动式"和"兼语式"为例，一般的汉语语法和对外汉语课本中都有所涉及，但本书就没有提到，因为类似的语法现象在英文中也有，学生在学习上没有任何困难，也没有必要了解过于细微的差别。

在具体语法点的解释上，我们的原则是少而精，点到为止。某一语法点的某些方面留到以后再讲，重复循环。

适当的英汉对比对学生理解两种语言的不同之处是有益的。

本书美方二人编委有何宝璋、胡文泽，参加本书编写工作的美方教师有（按姓名字母排序）陈珮嘉、胡文泽、李爱民、邱妙津。

在此感谢贾志杰老师为课文提供英文翻译，Nick Smith 先生对全书英文审定，戴晓雪、邓立立、陈念湘老师也为本书做了一些工作，孙静怡老师、万敏老师在试用期间提出了宝贵意见。并感谢哈佛大学 2000—2003 年三年间试用本书的初级汉语课的学生们。

何宝璋
2004 年 3 月

目　　录

第十六课　谈学习

16.1　课文（Text）

(1)

乔治：
Qiáozhì　Dàwèi　nǐ yǒu hǎo jǐ tiān méiyǒu gēn wǒmen yì qǐ dǎqiú le　máng
大卫，你 有 好 几 天 没有 跟 我们 一起 打球 了， 忙
shénme ne
什 么 呢?

大卫：
Dàwèi　Búshì zhǔnbèi kǎoshì　jiùshì zuò zuòyè　měi tiān de shìqíng zhème
不是 准备 考试，就是 做 作业，每 天 的 事情 这么
duō　nǎr yǒu shíjiān dǎqiú ne　Xià xīngqī yào jiāo de bàogào nǐ xiě
多，哪儿 有 时间 打球 呢? 下 星期 要 交 的 报告 你 写
wán le ma
完 了 吗?

乔治：
Qiáozhì　Xiě wán le　Nǐ ne
写 完 了。你 呢?

大卫：
Dàwèi　Kāishǐ xiě le　kěshì hái méiyǒu xiě wán ne　Duì le　něi tiān jiāo
开始 写 了，可是 还 没有 写 完 呢。对 了，哪天 交?
Xīngqī yī háishì xīngqī'èr
星 期一 还是 星期二?

乔治：
Qiáozhì　Xīngqī'èr　Nǐ kuài diǎnr xiě ba
星 期二，你 快 点儿 写 吧。

大卫：
Dàwèi　Wǒ zuò wán jīntiān Hànyǔ kè de fānyì liànxí jiù kāishǐ zuò　Fānyì liàn
我 做 完 今天 汉语课 的 翻译 练习 就 开始 做。翻译 练
xí nǐ zuò wán le ma
习 你 做 完 了 吗?

乔治：
Qiáozhì　Yígòng yào fānyì wǔ ge jùzi　wǒ yǐjīng fānyì le liǎng jù le　hái
一共 要 翻译 五个 句子，我 已经 翻译 了 两 句了，还

yǒu sān jù
有 三 句。

Dàwèi　Wǒ fānyì hǎo le yǐhòu　wǒmen yìqǐ tǎolùn tǎolùn ba
大卫： 我 翻译 好 了 以后， 我们 一起 讨论 讨论 吧。

Qiáozhì　Hǎo
乔治： 好。

(2)

Wǒ shì yì niánjí de xuéshēng　Wǒ de xuéxí bǐjiào jǐnzhāng　Zhège xuéqī wǒ yí
我 是 一 年级 的 学生。 我 的 学习 比较 紧张。 这个 学期 我 一

gòng xuǎn le sì-mén-kè　Chúle hànyǔ yǐwài　wǒ hái xuǎn le Zhōngguó lìshǐ shù
共 选 了 四 门 课。 除了 汉语 以外， 我 还 选 了 中 国 历史、数

xué hé jīngjì　Wǒ měi gè xīngqī yǒu shí sì jié kè　měi tiān dōu yǒu kè　Yīnwèi wǒ
学 和 经济。 我 每 个 星期 有 十四 节 课， 每 天 都 有 课。因为 我

shì yī niánjí de xuéshēng　suǒyǐ wǒ hái méiyǒu xuǎn zhuānyè　Wǒ xǐ huan jīngjì
是 一 年级 的 学 生 ， 所以 我 还 没有 选 专业。我 喜欢 经济，

dànshì wǒ duì Zhōngguó yě yǒu xìngqù　Wǒ xiǎng wǒ kěnéng xuǎn Dōngyà yánjiū
但是 我 对 中 国 也 有 兴趣。我 想 我 可 能 选 东亚 研究。

16.2　词语（Vocabulary）

1. 好几	hǎo jǐ		a couple, a few
2. 打球	dǎqiú	v.	to play ball
3. 忙	máng	v.; adj.	busy
4. 准备	zhǔnbèi	v.	to prepare
5. 考试	kǎoshì	n.	test, exam
6. 作业	zuòyè	n.	homework
7. 每天	měi tiān	phrase	everyday
8. 事情	shìqing	n.	thing, matter
9. 这么	zhème	adv.	so; such
10. 完	wán	v.	a complement used after verbs to indicate completion
11. 可是	kěshì	conj	but
12. 还是	háishì	conj.	or
13. 翻译	fānyì	v.; n.	to translate; translation
14. 句子	jùzi	n.	sentence
15. 句	jù	m. w.	measure word for sentences
16. 讨论	tǎolùn	v.	to discuss, to talk about
17. 年级	niánjí	n.	grade, year (in school)
18. 紧张	jǐnzhāng	adj.	nervous
19. 选	xuǎn	v.	to select, to enroll
20. 门	mén	m. w.	measure word for a course
21. 除了…以外	chúle…yǐwài	expr. pattern	except; besides
22. 历史	lìshǐ	n.	history
23. 数学	shùxué	n.	mathematics
24. 节	jié	m. w.	measure word for a class section
25. 因为	yīnwèi	conj.	because
26. 所以	suǒyǐ	conj.	so, therefore, as a result
27. 专业	zhuānyè	n.	specialty, major, concentration

28. 对…有兴趣	duì…yǒu xìngqù	v.	to be interested in
29. 可能	kěnéng	adv.	maybe, probably
30. 东亚	Dōngyà	n.	East Asia
31. 研究	yánjiū	v.; n.	research, study
32. 乔治	Qiáozhì	proper noun	George

16.3　注释（Notes）

1. 哪儿有时间打球呢?

在这样的反问句中，"哪儿"不是问什么地点或时间，而是通过反问后面所说事情的可能性表达强烈的否定。下面的句子与此相同：

In such rhetorical questions, 哪儿 is not used to refer to a place or time. Instead, it is used rhetorically to question the possibility of the following statement, indicating strong negation. Similar examples are：

我哪儿知道她喜欢不喜欢你?（How can I possibly know if she likes you or not?）

这个周末我要看三本书，写两个报告，哪儿有时间跟你去看电影呢?（This weekend I have to read three books and finish two papers. How can I possibly have time to go to the movies with you?）

2. 每（every）

"每"一般与量词一起使用，如"每个星期"、"每栋楼"、"每位客人"，但"每个人"中的"个"习惯上省略为"每人"，时间名词"天"、"年"前面直接加"每"，说"每天"、"每年"。

每 is usually used with a measure word, as in 每个星期（every week），每栋楼（every building），and 每位客人（every guest）. However, the measure word is often conventionally omitted with 人，每人（every person），and is fused with 天 and 年，每天（every day），每年（every year）.

为了强调，副词"都"和"每"配合使用。如：

For the purpose of emphasis，都 is often used with 每 together，as in：

老师每天都去办公室。(The teacher goes to the office every day.)

每个学中文的学生都有一个中文名字吗?(Does every student of Chinese have a Chinese name?)

3. S V *le* Num M N *le*

这个句型中,第一个"了"(*le*)标志 **V Num M N** 表示的动作行为的完结,第二个"了"(*le*)表明一个新的状况的确立,而这个新状况或与当前相关或是动作行为进行中的一个点或阶段。这种句型也称为部分完成句,表示至目前完成的数量,而且含有要继续进行的意思。例如:

The first *le*(了) in this pattern signals the completion of the action presented by **V Num M N**, while the second *le*(了) shows setting of a new situation, indicating current relevance or a point of progress. This pattern is also known as one for partial completion, meaning *this much has been accomplished so far*, and it implies that more is expected to follow. For example:

我们已经学了三百个汉字了。(We have already learned 300 characters so far.)

这个学期我们一共要写四个报告。现在我已经写了两个了。(This semester we need to write four papers altogether. I have finished two so far.)

16.4 语法(Grammar)

1. S 有 Duration 不/没 V

这个句型表示在一个时段里所说的动作行为不会或没有发生。例如:

This is a pattern to express the length of time that some event has not occurred. For example:

我有三个月没看电影了。(I haven't seen a movie for three months.)

下个星期大卫有两天不来上课,他要去日本打球。(Next week David will be absent for two days. He is going to play ball in Japan.)

这个句型里,"有"可以省略。如:

In this pattern, 有 can be omitted. For example:

玛丽好几个星期没给她妈妈打电话了。(Mary hasn't called her mother for quite a few weeks.)

2. 结果补语（Resultant complement）

结果补语（RC）由动词后面的一个词（一般是动词或形容词）或短语构成，指明动作行为的结果。动词＋补语（V＋RC）就像一个动词一样，可以带宾语，可以被"了"（*le*）或其他词语修饰。

A resultant complement（RC）is a word（normally a verb or an adjective）or a phrase that follows a verb to indicate the resulting state of the action. The combined form V＋RC is treated as a single verb, which can be modified by an object, *le*, or other words.

我们做完练习以后再看电视，好不好？(We'll watch TV after we finish doing the homework. Is that OK?)

红颜色的毛衣卖完了。你要黄色的吗？ (All the red sweaters have been sold out. Do you want a yellow one?)

那个字你们都写错了。(You all wrote that character wrong.)

动词与补语（V＋RC）一般情况不能分开，除非补语是可能补语。可能补语表示"能够达到某种结果"或"不能够达到某种结果"的意思，分别在动词（V）和补语（RC）之间加上"得"（*de*）和"不"（*bu*）构成。

The V and RC in this form cannot be separated except when used in potential expressions：*can*（or *cannot*）*achieve such a result*. Such potential expressions are made by inserting 得（positive）or 不（negative）between V and RC.

我今天<u>看得完</u>这本书，但是<u>写不完</u>那个报告。(Today I can finish reading this book, but I cannot finish writing that report.)

宫保鸡丁很难做，我<u>做不好</u>。(Kong-pao chicken is hard to make. I can't make it well.)

3. 除了 VP₁（O₁）以外，S 还 VP₂（O₂）

这是一个表示"补充"、"追加"的句型。

This is a sentence pattern which means *in addition to* A（VP$_1$（O$_1$）），S *also does* B （VP$_2$ （O$_2$））.

除了翻译句子以外，我还写了一个报告。（In addition to translating some sentences, I also wrote a report.）

在晚会上，除了唱歌以外我们还跳了舞。（In addition to singing, we also danced at the party.）

如果 VP$_1$ 与 VP$_2$ 是同一个主语，S 可以放到 VP$_1$ 前面，如：
In this pattern, the subject S can appear before VP$_1$, for example,

在晚会上，我们除了唱歌以外还跳了舞。（In addition to singing, we also danced at the party.）

乔治除了学习汉语以外，还学习中国历史。（In addition to the Chinese language, George is also learning Chinese history.）

如果 VP$_1$ 和 VP$_2$ 中的动词相同，VP$_1$ 里的动词可以省略。如：
If the verbs in VP$_1$ and VP$_2$ are the same, the verb in VP$_1$ can be omitted. For example,

乔治除了汉语以外，还学习中国历史。（In addition to the Chinese language, George is also learning Chinese history.）

4. 因为…所以…

"因为 P，所以 Q" 可以译成英语句子 *because P, Q* 或 *P, therefore Q*。要注意的是，在英语中 *because*（因为）和 *therefore*（所以）不同时出现在一个句子里，但是汉语中"因为"和"所以"同时出现在一个句子里是典型的用法。

'因为 P，所以 Q'can be translated into English as *because P, Q*, or as *P, therefore Q*. What needs to be noted is that, while in English *because* and *therefore* are normally not present in the same sentence, but in Chinese 因为 and 所以 typically are.

因为你还没做完作业，所以你现在不可以去打球。（You haven't finished doing your homework yet, therefore you may not go and play ball now.）

因为我睡觉睡到中午才起来，所以我没吃早饭。（I didn't have breakfast because I didn't get up till noon.)

"因为"可以省略，表示较弱的因果推理，如：

In a weak inference，因为 can be omitted, as in,

我还没做完作业，所以不能和你去打球。(I haven't finished my homework yet，therefore I can not play ball with you.)

16.5 翻译（Translation）

Lesson Sixteen：Talking about Studying

（1）

George：David, you haven't played ball with us for quite a few days. What are you busy doing?

David：I am either preparing for an exam or doing homework. There is so much to do everyday. How can I possibly have time to play ball? Have you finished the paper we are supposed to submit next week?

George：Yes, I have. How about you?

David：I have started, but I haven't finished writing it. Oh yes, when are we supposed to turn it in? Monday or Tuesday?

George：Tuesday. You'd better hurry up.

David：As soon as I am done with the translation exercise for the Chinese class today, I will get started. Are you done with your translation exercise?

George：There are five sentences to translate all together. I have done two of them. There are three more left.

David：After I am done with the translation, let's get together and talk about it.

George：OK.

（2）

I am a freshman. My studies are intense. Altogether I am taking four courses this semester. In addition to Chinese, I am also taking history, mathematics and economics. I have fourteen hours of class every week and I have classes every day. Because I am a freshman, I haven't selected a major yet. I like economics, but I am also interested in China. I think I will probably take East Asian Studies.

第十七课　在邮局

17.1　课文（Text）

（1）（大卫在邮局里（David is in the post office））

Dàwèi　Xiǎojiě　wǒ yào jì liǎng fēng xìn　zhèi fēng jì dào Shànghǎi　zhè fēng
大卫：小姐，我要寄两封信，这封寄到上海，这封

jì dào Niǔyuē
寄到纽约。

Gōngzuòrényuán　Zhèi fēng bā máo　Qǐng xiě shàng shōuxìnrén de yóuzhèng
工作人员：这封八毛。请写上收信人的邮政

biānmǎ
编码。

Dàwèi　Wǒ bù zhīdào yóuzhèng biānmǎ shì duōshǎo
大卫：我不知道邮政编码是多少。

Gōngzuòrényuán　Nǐ kěyǐ qù nàbiān chá yíxià
工作人员：你可以去那边查一下。（point at a place）

（邮局工作人员称信的重量（The clerk is weighing the letter to New York））

Gōngzuòrényuán　Zhèi fēng guó jì hángkōngxìn chāozhòng le　yào tiē liù kuài
工作人员：这封国际航空信超重了，要贴六块

sì de yóupiào
四的邮票。

Dàwèi　Zài mǎi wǔ zhāng bā máo de yóupiào hé shí zhāng Běijīng de fēngjǐng
大卫：再买五张八毛的邮票和十张北京的风景

míngxìnpiàn
明信片。

Gōngzuòrényuán　Yígòng èr shí yī kuài èr
工作人员：一共二十一块二。

（写上邮政编码贴好邮票后，大卫把信交给邮局工作人员 （After writing down the zip code and putting on the stamp, David gives the letter to the clerk））

Dàwèi　nǐ hǎo　gěi nǐ
大卫：你 好， 给 你。

Gōngzuòrényuán　Qǐng fàng jìn wàibiān de yóutǒng lǐ
　工 作 人 员：请 放 进 外边 的 邮 筒 里。

（2）

Zài Zhōngguó dì yī cì zǒu jìn yóujú de shíhòu　nǐ huì fāxiàn Zhōngguó de yóu
在 中 国 第一次 走 进 邮局 的 时候， 你 会 发现 中 国 的 邮
jú gēn Měiguó de yóujú hěn bù yíyàng　Búdàn kěyǐ jì shū　jì xìn　jì bāoguǒ　yě
局 跟 美国 的 邮局 很 不 一样。不但 可以 寄书、寄信、寄包裹，也
kěyǐ mǎi yóupiào　xìnfēng hé míngxìnpiàn　érqiě hái kěyǐ dìng bàozhǐ　zázhì dǎ
可以 买 邮票、信 封 和 明 信 片，而且 还 可以 订 报 纸、杂志，打
diànhuà děngděng
电 话 等 等。

Yóujú suīrán hěn fāngbiàn dànshì xiànzài diànnǎo zhème fādá hěn duō yǐqián
邮局 虽然 很 方 便，但是 现 在 电 脑 这 么 发 达，很 多 以 前
zhǐyǒu dào yóujú cái néng zuò de shìqíng xiànzài zài jiā lǐ dōu kěyǐ zuò le Rénrén
只有 到 邮 局 才 能 做 的 事 情，现 在 在 家 里 都 可 以 做 了。人 人
dōu yòng diànzǐ yóujiàn hé chuánzhēn Zhēn bù zhīdào yǐhòu shìfǒu hái huì
都 用 电子 邮 件 和 传 真 。 真 不 知 道 以 后 是 否 还 会
yǒu yóujú
有 邮局。

17.2 词语（Vocabulary）

1.	邮局	yóujú	n.	post office
2.	寄信	jìxìn	v.	to send mail
3.	收信人	shōuxìnrén	n.	receiver, addressee
4.	邮政编码	yóuzhèng biānmǎ	phrase	zip code
5.	那边	nèibiān/nàbiān	dem. pron.	there
6.	查	chá	v.	to check, to look up
7.	航空信	hángkōngxìn	n.	international airmail
8.	超重	chāozhòng	v.	to overweigh
9.	贴	tiē	v.	to paste
10.	邮票	yóupiào	n.	stamp
11.	再	zài	adv.	again, once more
12.	风景	fēngjǐng	n.	scenery, landscape
13.	明信片	míngxìnpiàn	n.	postcard
14.	放进	fàngjìn	v.	to put in
15.	邮筒	yóutǒng	n.	mailbox
16.	次	cì	m. w.	time; measure word for re-peatable events
17.	会	huì	modal verb	will, may
18.	发现	fāxiàn	v.; n.	to find, to discover
19.	一样	yíyàng	adj.	the same
20.	不但	búdàn	conj.	not only
21.	包裹	bāoguǒ	n.	parcel, package
22.	而且	érqiě	conj.	moreover, furthermore

23. 订	dìng	v.	to book, to reserve, to subscribe
24. 报纸	bàozhǐ	n.	newspaper
25. 杂志	zázhì	n.	magazine
26. 等等	děngděng	particle	and so on, etc.
27. 方便	fāngbiàn	adj.	convenient
28. 电脑	diànnǎo	n.	computer
29. 发达	fādá	adj.	developed, advanced
30. 只有	zhǐyǒu	conj.	only
31. 才	cái	adv.	only
32. 能	néng	modal verb	to be able to; to be permitted by circumstance
33. 都	dōu	adv.	all
34. 人人	rénrén		everyone
35. 电子邮件	diànzǐ yóujiàn	phrase	email
36. 传真	chuánzhēn	n.	facsimile, fax
37. 是否	shìfǒu	adv.	if; whether
38. 上海	Shànghǎi	proper noun	Shanghai
39. 纽约	Niǔyuē	proper noun	New York
40. 北京	Běijīng	proper noun	Beijing

17.3　注释（Notes）

1. 寄到，写上，放进

这些都是"动词＋补语"的形式：

These are all V＋RC forms：

寄＋到上海　　　　写＋上（信封）　　　　放 ＋ 进 信筒

mail＋ to Shanghai, write ＋ onto（the envelope）, put＋into the mailbox

2. 再买五张八毛的邮票

这里的"再"表示在已经做的事情以外有补充或增加。

再 here means *then* or *in addition*.

3. 等等 vs. 什么的

"等等"是比较正式的表达形式，日常谈话和正式文字里都可以使用，而"什么的"是一个口语用的表达形式，不用在正式的谈话和文字里。

等等 is a formal expression, which can be used in both daily speech and formal writings, while 什么的 is an informal spoken expression.

"等等"和"什么的"在用法上也有所不同。

They are also different in terms of usage.

"等等"多用来列举同类事物或人：

等等：list members of the same kind：

这家商店卖的毛衣颜色真多，有红的，黄的，绿的，蓝的，等等。
我的好朋友都来参加我的晚会了，大卫，玛丽，乔治等等都来了。

"什么的"多用来列举不同类的事物（不能用于人），有诸如此类的意思：

什么的：list different kinds of things, meaning *things like that*（it should not be used to refer to people）：

这家小卖部卖信纸、信封、本子、铅笔什么的。

17.4　语法（Grammar）

1. A 跟 B（不）一样

这是一个说明 A 与 B 相同或不相同的句型。在这个句型里，A 和 B 可以是名词短语、动词短语或小句。

This is a sentence pattern for saying *A and B are the same or not the same*. In this pattern, A and B can be noun phrases, verb phrases or clauses.

A 和 B 是名词短语（Noun phrase）：
你的书跟我的书一样。（Your book is the same as mine.）

A 和 B 是动词短语（Verb phrase）：
说中国话跟唱中国歌很不一样。（Speaking Chinese is very different from sing-

ing in Chinese.)

A 和 B 是小句（Clauses）：
<u>中国学生学英文</u>跟<u>美国学生学中文</u>不太一样。（A Chinese student's way of learning English is not the same as an American student's way of learning Chinese）.

2. 不但…而且…
"不但…而且…"在意思和用法上与英语的 not only... but also... 十分相似：
This pattern is very similar to the English expression *not only... but also...* in meaning and in usage：

在中国的邮局，你<u>不但</u>可以寄信，<u>而且</u>可以订报纸。（In a post office in China, you can *not only* mail letters, *but* you can *also* subscribe to newspapers. ）
<u>不但</u>北京人知道王府井，<u>而且</u>留学生也都知道王府井在哪儿。（*Not only* Beijing people know Wangfujing, foreign students *also* know where it is. ）

3. 只有…才…
这个语型构成"只有 A 才 B"，其中，"A"是实现或达到"B"必须满足的条件或环境。"才"后面多跟着"能"、"能够"、"可以"等。
This is a pattern used to say that *something can be achieved only when certain conditions are met*, or *only under certain circumstances can something be achieved.*

<u>只有</u>在中国<u>才</u>能买到这本字典。（Only in China can one get a copy of this dictionary. ）
你<u>只有</u>每天练习<u>才</u>能学好中文。（You can learn Chinese well only by practicing every day. ）
他爸爸说，他<u>只有</u>做完了练习<u>才可以</u>看电视。（His father said that he may watch TV only after he has finished doing his homework. ）

4. <u>人人都 V</u>
"人人"由"人"重叠构成，表示"每个人"。单音节量词、一些单音节名词和时间名词可以重叠，表示遍指该集合的所有元素，意思相当于"每…"（*every...* , *all...*）。如：

人人 is reduplication of 人 meaning *everybody* or *every person*. Reduplicated usages of Mono-syllabic measure words and some mono-syllabic common nouns as well as time words suggest a uniform coverage of all the elements of a set, meaning *every-y...*, *all...*. For example,

个个（*每个*）　　　家家（*每家*）　　　封封（*每封*）

天天（*每天*）　　　年年（*每年*）　　　月月（*每月*）

N MM 都 V

这个学校的女生<u>个个</u>都很漂亮。（The girls in this school are all very pretty.）

我这个学期选的课<u>门门</u>都很有意思。（Every course that I am taking this semester is interesting.）

这儿的大学<u>个个</u>都有名。（All the universities here are famous.）

5. 嵌入的正反问句（Embedded *yes-no* questions）

正反问充当句子成分，可以有两种形式。

A yes-no question can be embedded in a sentence in one of the two ways.

（1）用"肯定＋否定"（*V-not-V*）形式：

Using the V-not-V form：

我不知道老师今天<u>来不来</u>。（I don't know if the teacher will come or not.）

大卫问邮局的工作人员他的信<u>超重没超重</u>。（David asked the post office staff if his letter was overweight.）

（2）用"是否＋动词"（是否＋*V*）形式：

Using 是否：

大卫不知道他要寄的信<u>是否超重</u>。（David didn't know if the letter he wanted mailed was overweight or not.）

大卫想知道乔治<u>是否认识</u>玛丽。（David wanted to know if George knew Mary or not.）

17.5 翻译（Translation）

Lesson Seventeen   In the Post Office

（1）（David is in the post office）

David：Miss, I have two letters to send. This one goes to Shanghai and this one to New York.

Clerk：Eighty cents for this one. Please write down the addressee's zip code.

David：I don't know the zip code.

Clerk：（pointing at a place）You can look it up over there.

（The clerk is weighing the letter to New York）

Clerk：This international airmail weighs more than the standard weight. It takes a 6-*kuai*-4-*mao* stamp.

David：I'd like to buy five 8-mao stamps and ten of the postcards with Beijing scenery.

Clerk：They come to a total of 21 *kuai* and 2 *mao*.

（After writing down the zip code and putting on the stamp, David gives the letter to the clerk）

David：Hello again. Here you are.

Clerk：Please drop it into the mailbox outside.

（2）

When you walk into a post office in China for the first time, you will notice how different the Chinese post office is from a post office in America. You can not only send books, letters and parcels by mail, but you can also buy stamps, envelopes and postcards. You can even subscribe to newspapers and magazines, make phone calls, and so on.

The post office is a convenient place, but with computers so advanced, people may now do things at home that they could only do in a post office before. Everybody is using email and fax machines. It is hard to tell if post offices are going to be around any more in the future.

第十八课 谈天气

18.1 课文（Text）

（1）（大卫和乔治下课后在聊天儿（David is chatting with George after a class））

Dàwèi Jīntiān zhēn lěng
大卫：今天 真 冷。

Qiáozhì Shì a dōngtiān kuàiyào lái le
乔治：是 啊，冬 天 快 要 来 了。

Dàwèi Běijīng qiūtiān de tiānqì zhēn hǎo
大卫：北 京 秋 天 的 天 气 真 好。

Qiáozhì Dōu shì qíngtiān jì bù lěng yě bú rè
乔治：都 是 晴 天，既 不 冷 也 不 热。

Dàwèi Dōngtiān zěnmeyàng
大卫：冬 天 怎 么 样？

Qiáozhì Běijīng dōngtiān hěn gānzào bú xià yǔ yě hěn shǎo xià xuě hái
乔治：北 京 冬 天 很 干 燥，不 下 雨，也 很 少 下 雪，还
chángcháng guā dà fēng
常 常 刮 大 风。

Dàwèi Zhēn zāogāo Nǐ zhīdào míngtiān de tiānqì zěnmeyàng ma
大卫：真 糟 糕。你 知 道 明 天 的 天 气 怎 么 样 吗？

Qiáozhì Tiānqì yùbào shuō míngtiān báitiān duōyún zhuǎn yīn dōngběifēng
乔治：天 气 预 报 说，明 天 白 天 多 云 转 阴，东 北 风
sì dào wǔ jí zuì gāo qìwēn shísì dù
四 到 五 级，最 高 气 温 十 四 度。

（看看表（Taking a look at his watch））

Qiáozhì Kuài yào shàngkè le wǒmen jìn jiàoshì ba
乔治：快 要 上 课 了，我 们 进 教 室 吧。

今天真冷。

是啊，冬天快要来了。

(2)

Běijīng yì nián sìjì de tiānqì   chūntiān hé qiūtiān zuì hǎo   jì bù lěng yě bú
北京 一 年 四季 的 天气， 春天 和 秋天 最 好， 既 不 冷 也 不

rè fēicháng shūfu   Zuìjìn jǐ nián Běijīng de xiàtiān fēicháng rè   érqiě rè de shí
热，非常 舒服。最近 几 年 北京 的 夏天 非常 热，而且 热 的 时

jiān yě bǐjiào cháng   Běijīng de dōngtiān hěn lěng   hěnshǎo xiàxuě dànshì cháng
间 也 比较 长 。北京 的 冬天 很 冷， 很 少 下雪 但是 常

guā dà fēng   yòu lěng yòu gānzào   wǒ fēicháng bù xǐhuān
刮 大 风 ，又 冷 又 干燥，我 非常 不 喜欢 。

18.2 词语（Vocabulary）

1. 天气	tiānqì	n.	weather
2. 冷	lěng	adj.	cold
3. 冬天	dōngtiān	n.	winter
4. 快要	kuàiyào	adv.	about to, almost

5. 秋天	qiūtiān	n.	autumn, fall
6. 晴天	qíngtiān	n.	sunny day
7. 既不… 也不…	jìbù… yěbù…	expr. pattern	neither... nor...
8. 热	rè	adj.	hot
9. 干燥	gānzào	adj.	dry
10. 下雨	xiàyǔ	v.	to rain
11. 很少	hěnshǎo	adv.	seldom
12. 下雪	xiàxuě	v.	to snow
13. 刮风	guāfēng	v.	to blow (wind), windy
14. 糟糕	zāogāo	adj.	awful
15. 预报	yùbào	n.	forecast
16. 白天	báitiān	n.	daytime
17. 多云	duōyún	adj.	cloudy
18. 转阴	zhuǎnyīn	v.	to turn darkly cloudy or overcast
19. 东北风	dōngběifēng	n.	northeastern wind
20. 到	dào	prep.	to (used in defining a range)
21. 级	jí	n.	level
22. 最	zuì	adv.	most
23. 气温	qìwēn	n.	temperature
24. 度	dù	n.	degree (temperature)
25. 四季	sìjì	n.	four seasons
26. 春天	chūntiān	n.	spring
27. 非常	fēicháng	adv.	very, extraordinarily
28. 最近	zuìjìn	n.	recent, recently
29. 夏天	xiàtiān	n.	summer
30. 长	cháng	adj.	long
31. 又…又…	yòu…yòu…	expr. pattern	not only... but also...

18.3 注释（Notes）

1. 四到五级

这里的"到"用来指出范围的起、止。下面是另外一些例子：

到 is used here to specify a range. More examples：

一年级到三年级的学生（students from the first to the third-year）

六十岁到八十岁的老人（elders from 60 to 80 years old）

老师下午两点到四点在办公室。（The teacher is in her office from 2 to 4 pm.）

2. 秋天最好

"最"用在形容词或某些动词前面表示程度的最高级：

最 is used before an adjective or some verbs to act as a superlative, such as *most* or *best*：

最高的楼（the tallest building）

最好的学校（the best school）

最难的一课（the most difficult lesson）

我最喜欢蓝色的毛衣。（I like blue sweaters best.）

3. 而且

"而且"表示在前面所说情况的基础上"进一步"或"深一层"的意思。

而且 means *further more* or *on top of that*.

王山的宿舍很小，也很贵，而且离学校很远。（Wang Shan's dorm is small and expensive. On top of that, it is far from the school.）

学汉字很有用，而且很有意思。（Learning Chinese characters is useful, and it is interesting, too.）

4. 很少

"很少"用作形容词时，通常只做谓语，不单独做定语：

When used as an adjective, 很少 can usually be used as a predicate, not as a modifier alone：

他这个人兴趣不多，朋友<u>也</u><u>很少</u>。（＊他有很少朋友 would be incorrect）

"很少"用作副词时，用在动词前面，表示动词所说事情发生的频率非常低：
When used as an adverb，很少 means *seldom or rarely* and is used before verbs：

我的同屋<u>很少</u>去图书馆。（My roommate seldom goes to the library. ）
那儿<u>很少</u>下雪。（It rarely snows there. ）
这个学期我太忙了，<u>很少</u>打球。（I have been too busy this semester. I seldom play ball. ）

18.4　语法（Grammar）

1.（快）要 V 了
这里的"要"表示时间离 V 表示事情的发生很近了，近似于英语的 *about to happen* 或 *will happen soon*。
　　要 in this usage is used to express the imminence of an event, meaning *something is about to happen* or *something will happen soon.*

他的女朋友<u>要</u>来哈佛看他了。（His girlfriend will come to Harvard to visit him soon. ）

"快"用来强调"时间离 V 表示事情的发生很近"的意思：
快 is used here to stress the shortness to the time when action V expressed：

新年<u>快要</u>到了。（The New Year is coming soon. ）
新学期<u>快要</u>开始了。（The new semester will start soon. ）

2. 既不…也不…
这个语型表示对并列两个动词短语的否定，与英语的 *neither... nor...* 相似，不同在于 *neither... nor...* 可以对并列两个名词短语的否定（如，*neither David nor his roommate...*），而这个语型不能。

如果我是老师，我就不要学生考试。

在推理较弱的句子里，可以不用"就"。例如：

However, if the inference between condition and its result is a weak inference, 就 is not needed. For example：

如果我有时间，我一定给你写信。
如果你想找她，我可以给你她的电话号码。
如果玛丽不来，你会来吗？

19.5　翻译（Translation）

Lesson Nineteen　Taking a Taxi

（1）（David gets into a taxi at the gate of the university）

Driver：Hi. Where to?

David：The Beijing Train Station. Can you tell me how long it takes to get there?

Driver：At least 40 minutes. The traffic is jammed everywhere at the moment.

David：It took me an hour and half last time to get to the Palace Museum by bus.

Driver：Where are you from? How long have you been in China?

David：I am American. I have been in China for three months.

Driver：Have you gotten used to your life in Beijing?

David：Not yet.

Driver：You will eventually.

Driver：This is the Beijing Train Station. 27 *kuai*.

David：（taking out 21 *kuai* and handing it to the driver）Here is your 21 *kuai*.

Driver：（slowly）It is 27 *kuai*.

David：Sorry. I thought it was 21 *kuai*.

Drive：That's OK.

David：Can you give me a receipt please?

Driver：Sure.

（2）

The public traffic system in Beijing is convenient. There are many taxis and buses. It is cheap to take the bus, but it's slow. Sometimes you have to change buses. A taxi is faster than the bus, but it is more expensive than the bus. I don't like to take the bus, nor do I like to take a taxi. If where I am going is not far, I either walk or ride a bike. It not only saves money, but it is also exercise. I may meet a Chinese person on my way and we can talk while we walk. In this way, I can practice my Chinese as well as learn about China.

第二十课　接朋友

20.1　课文（Text）

（1）（欧文和王林在北京站出口还没等到大卫（Owen and Wang Lin can't find David at the exit of the Beijing Train Station））

WángLín　Nǐ péngyou zhīdào nǐ dào Běijīng de shíjiān ma　Tā zhǎo de dào nǐ
王　林：你 朋 友 知道 你 到 北京 的 时间 吗？他 找 得 到 你
　　　　ma
　　　　吗？.

Ōuwén　Zhīdào　Wǒ pà tā zhǎo bú dào　zuótiān gěi tā dǎ le diànhuà
欧文：知道。我 怕 他 找 不 到，昨天 给 他 打 了 电 话。

你朋友知道你到北京的时间吗？

知道。

（五分钟后大卫到了（David arrives 5 minutes later））

Dàwèi　Wéi　Ōuwén
大卫：喂，欧文。

Ōuwén　Nǐ hǎo
欧文：你好。

Dàwèi　Duìbuqǐ　wǒ qù cèsuǒ le　Děng duō jiǔ le
大卫：对不起，我去厕所了。等多久了？

Ōuwén　Chàbuduō wǔ fēnzhōng　Wǒ lái gěi nǐmen jièshào yíxià
欧文：差不多五分钟。我来给你们介绍一下：

　　　　Zhèi wèi shì Wáng Lín xiānsheng　zài Běijīng yì jiā shípǐn gōngsī
（To David）这位是王林先生，在北京一家食品公司

　　　　gōngzuò
　　　　工作。

　　　　Zhè shì Dàwèi　wǒ zài Měiguó de zhōngxué tóngxué
（To Wang Lin）这是大卫，我在美国的中学同学。

Wánglín　Nǐ hǎo
王林：你好。

Dàwèi　Nǐ hǎo
大卫：你好。

Ōuwén　Wáng xiānsheng qù Shànghǎi chūchāi　wǒmen shì zài huǒchē shàng rèn
欧文：王先生去上海出差，我们是在火车上认
　　　　shí de
　　　　识的。

Wánglín　Zhè shì wǒ de míngpiàn　shàngmiàn yǒu wǒ de diànhuà hé dì zhǐ
王林：这是我的名片，上面有我的电话和地址。
　　　　Huānyíng guānglín
　　　　欢迎光临。

Dàwèi　Xièxie　Wǒ de diànhuà shì 32517685　yě huānyíng nǐ qù wánr
大卫：谢谢。我的电话是32517685，也欢迎你去玩儿。

（2）

Zuótiān shì xīng qī liù　Mǎ lì cóngzǎodàowǎn máng le yì tiān　Tiān hái méiyǒu
昨天是星期六，玛丽从早到晚忙了一天。天还没有
liàng tā jiù qù fēi jī chǎng le　yīnwèi tā de péngyou yào zuò zǎoshàng de fēi jī dào
亮她就去飞机场了，因为她的朋友要坐早上的飞机到

Běijīng lái Kěshì fēi jī wǎndiǎn Mǎ lì zài nà lǐ děng le liǎng gè duō xiǎoshí Jiē
北 京 来。可 是，飞 机 晚 点，玛 丽 在 那 里 等 了 两 个 多 小 时。接
dào péngyou de shíhou yǐ jīng kuài shí diǎn le Tā péi péngyou dào le lǚguǎn bàn
到 朋 友 的 时 候 已 经 快 十 点 了。她 陪 朋 友 到 了 旅 馆，办
le zhùsù shǒuxù Zhōngwǔ tāmen yìbiān chīfàn yìbiān liáotiān liáo de hěn gāo
了 住 宿 手 续。 中 午 他 们 一 边 吃 饭 一 边 聊 天，聊 得 很 高
xìng
兴。

　　Tāmen tán dào bì yè yǐ hòu gè rén de shēnghuó gōngzuò hé xué xí   hái tán dào
　　他 们 谈 到 毕 业 以 后 各 人 的 生 活、工 作 和 学 习，还 谈 到
biéde tóngxué hé péngyou Xiàwǔ Mǎ lì dài tā de péngyou zuò dì tiě yóulǎn le Běi
别 的 同 学 和 朋 友。下 午 玛 丽 带 她 的 朋 友 坐 地 铁 游 览 了 北
jīngchéng
京 城。

20.2　词语（Vocabulary）

1. 怕	pà	v.	afraid
2. 厕所	cèsuǒ	n.	restroom
3. 等	děng	v.	to wait
4. 多久	duō jiǔ	phrase	how long...
5. 差不多	chàbuduō	adj.	about, nearly
6. 介绍	jièshào	v.	to introduce
7. 食品	shípǐn	n.	food
8. 公司	gōngsī	n.	company
9. 出差	chūchāi	v.	to be on a business trip
10. 名片	míngpiàn	n.	name card
11. 上面	shàngmiàn	n.	above, on top of
12. 地址	dìzhǐ	n.	address
13. 欢迎光临	huānyíng guānglín	phrase	Welcome!
14. 从早到晚	cóngzǎodàowǎn	phrase	from morning until night
15. 天亮	tiānliàng	v.	daybreak
16. 飞机场	fēijīchǎng	n.	airport
17. 飞机	fēijī	n.	airplane
18. 晚点	wǎndiǎn	v.	late, behind schedule

19. 接	jiē	v.	to pick (someone) up, to meet
20. 陪	péi	v.	to accompany
21. 旅馆	lǚguǎn	n.	hotel
22. 住宿	zhùsù	v.	to stay the night
23. 手续	shǒuxù	n.	procedure
24. 毕业	bìyè	v.	to graduate
25. 各人	gè rén	n.	each individual
26. 带	dài	v.	to bring
27. 地铁	dìtiě	n.	subway
28. 游览	yóulǎn	v.	to go sightseeing
29. 北京城	Běijīngchéng	n.	Beijing City

20.3　注释（Notes）

1. 欢迎光临

"欢迎光临"是客人到达时主人向客人表示欢迎的客套话。本课中，用来对朋友以后的来访表示欢迎，相当于对朋友的邀请。

Welcome!（lit. *Welcome, your honorable presence*!）This formulaic expression is typically used by the host or hostess upon their guest's arrival. In this lesson, it is used to extend a future invitation to a new friend, meaning *Welcome to visit my place when it is convenient for you to do so.*

2. 她的朋友要坐早上的飞机来

"要"在不同的上下文里可以表示不同的意思。这个句子里，"要"的意思是"将"，表示按照时间安排很快发生。下面是"要"表示不同意思的例句：

要 can have different meanings in different contexts. In this sentence, 要 means *to be going to*. The following are some examples of its various uses：

明天要下雨。（It is going to rain tomorrow.）
我要回家。（I want to go home.）
我明天要早一点起来。（I need to get up a little earlier tomorrow.）
你有问题要问老师。（If you have questions, you should ask the teacher.）
从宿舍走到学校要二十分钟。（It takes 20 minutes to walk from the dorm to the

school.）

我下学期学不学汉语<u>要</u>看我有没有时间。（Whether I will learn Chinese or not next semester <u>will</u> depend on whether I have time.）

3. 各人

"各人"相当于英语的 *each person*，"各"强调全体中个体间的区别，而"每人"相当于英语的 *every person*，"每"强调所有个体构成的整体。例如：

各人 means *each person*, emphasizing the distinction between units. 每人 means *every person*, connoting inclusion. For example：

<u>每</u>个学中文的人都有中文名字，但是<u>各</u>人的名字不一样。（Every student learning Chinese has a Chinese name, but each person's name is different from the others'.）

Normally, a measure word is needed between 各 and the noun it takes, such as 各位老师（*each teacher*），各个学校（*each school*），各个国家（*each country*）. But the measure word can be dropped if the noun is monosyllabic：各人，各校 and 各国.

20.4　语法（Grammar）

1. 时段的表达（Expression of duration）

"时段"表示动作行为或事件持续的时间长度，"时点"表示一个时间上的一个点。"时点"在句子中的位置一般是在谓语的前面，而"时段"在句子里典型的位置在谓语动词后面。

An expression of duration specifies how long an action or an event lasts. Different from an expression of punctual time, which always goes before the predicate of the sentence, an expression of duration typically comes after the verb.

S V Duration

玛丽昨天忙了一天。

她在飞机场等了两个多小时。

当句子里谓语动词后有宾语时，时段的使用有以下两种方式：

When an object is involved, the durational expression can take one of the two forms：

（1）S V Duration（的）O

我昨天打了<u>两个小时的</u>电话。（I was on the phone for two hours yesterday.）

他在哈佛学了<u>三年的</u>中文。（He studied Chinese for three years at Harvard.）

（2）S V－O V Duration

我们昨天晚上吃饭吃了<u>一个半小时</u>，聊天又聊了<u>两个小时</u>。（Last night we ate our meal for an hour and half and chatted for another two hours.）

欧文星期天在宿舍看电视看了<u>四个小时</u>。（Owen watched TV for four hours in his dorm on Sunday.）

2. 从…到…

"从…到…"通过指定起点和终点表示一个范围，与英语的 from... to... 相同：

This expression is used in exactly the same way as *from... to...* is used in English to define a range by specifying the two end points.

我们<u>从</u>星期一<u>到</u>星期五都有中文课。（We have Chinese classes from Monday through Friday.）

<u>从</u>上海<u>到</u>纽约的中国人都用汉字。（From Shanghai to New York, Chinese people all use characters.）

20.5   翻译（Translation）

Lesson Twenty   Meeting a Friend at the Train Station

（1）（Owen and Wang Lin can't find David at the exit of the Beijing Train Station.）

Wang Lin：Does your friend know your arrival time? Can he find you?

Owen：He does. Since I was afraid that he would not be able to find me, I called him yesterday.

（David arrives 5 minutes later.）

David：Hi, Owen.

Owen：Hi.

David：Sorry, I went to the restroom. How long have you been waiting?

Owen：About five minutes. Let me introduce you to each other.

（To David）This is Mr. Wang Lin. He works in a food company in Beijing.

（To Wang Lin）This is David, my middle school classmate from the United
　　　States.

Wang Lin：Hi.

David：Hi.

Owen：Mr. Wang was in Shanghai on business. We got to know each on the
　　　train.

Wang Lin：This is my name card. It has my phone number and address on it.
　　　　　You are welcome to visit me.

David：Thank you. My phone number is 3251－7685. Come and visit me too.

（2）

　　It was Saturday yesterday. Mary was busy all day. She went to the airport when
it was still dark because her friend was coming on an early morning flight to Beijing.
But the flight was late, so Mary waited there for over two hours. It was already close
to ten o'clock when she met her friend. She went with her friend to the hotel and
checked in. At noon, they had a chat while they were having lunch. They had a good
time talking with each other.

　　They each talked about their lives, jobs and their studies after their graduation.
They also talked about their classmates and friends. In the afternoon, Mary showed
her friend around the city of Beijing by subway.

第二十一课　找修理工

21.1　课文（Text）

（1）

Dàwèi　Wéi　fúwùtái ma
大卫：喂，服务台吗？

Fúwùyuán　Shìde　nín yǒu shénme shì
服务员：是的，您 有 什么 事？

Dàwèi　Wǒ shì 605 fángjiān de dàwèi　Wǒ fángjiān lǐ de dàdēng huài le　qǐng
大卫：我 是 605 房 间 的 大卫。我 房 间 里 的 大灯 坏 了，请

lái xiū lǐ yíxià
来 修理 一下。

Fúwùyuán　Diàngōng xiànzài bú zài　Tā xiàwǔ qù nǐ de fángjiān　hǎo ma
服务员：电工 现在 不在。他 下午 去 你 的 房 间，好 吗？

Dàwèi　Hǎo
大卫：好 。

（大卫下午四点又打电话（David calls again at 4：00 p. m.））

Dàwèi　Shì fúwùyuán ma
大卫：是 服务 员 吗？

Fúwùyuán　Duì　Shénme shì
服务员：对。什么 事？

Dàwèi　Wǒ de dēng huài le　shàngwǔ wǒ dǎ le diànhuà le　Nǐmen shuō diàn
大卫：我 的 灯 坏 了， 上午 我 打 了 电话 了。你们 说 电

gōng shīfu xiàwǔ láixiū　Xiànzài dōu sì diǎn le　tā hái méi lái
工 师傅下午 来修。 现在 都 四 点 了，他 还 没 来。

Fúwùyuán　Zhēn duìbuqǐ　diàngōng xiàwǔ yìzhí hěn máng　Tā wǔ diǎn yǐqián
服务员：真 对不起， 电工 下午 一直 很 忙。他 五 点 以前

kěndìng huì dào nǐ fángjiān
肯定 会 到 你 房 间。

（大卫听见有人敲门（David hears a knock on the door））

Dàwèi　　　　　　　Qǐng jìn
大 卫：（opens the door）请 进。

Diàngōng　Dēng zěnme la
电 工：灯 怎么 啦?

Dàwèi　Jīntiān zǎoshàng tūrán miè le
大卫：今天 早 上 突然 灭 了。

Diàngōng　Ràng wǒ kàn kan
电 工：让 我 看 看。

（电工查看灯泡（The electrician looks at the light bulb））

Diàngōng　Dēngpào huài le　huàn yí gè
电 工：灯 泡 坏 了, 换 一 个。

（电工换了灯泡（He replaces it））

Diàngōng　Xiànzài hǎo le　qǐng kāi dēng
电 工：现 在 好 了，请 开 灯。

（大卫合上开关，灯亮了（David turns the switch on. The light is on））

Dàwèi　Liàng le　Xièxie nín
大卫：亮 了。谢谢 您。

Diàngōng　Búyòng xiè
电 工：不 用 谢。

(2)

Zìxíngchē zài Zhōngguó shì yì zhǒng hěn zhòngyào de jiāotōnggōngjù　jī hū
自行车 在 中 国 是 一 种 很 重 要 的 交 通 工具，几乎
jiājiā dōu yǒu　lián wàiguó liúxuéshēng dào Zhōngguó hòu yě mǎi zìxíngchē qí　Dà
家家 都 有，连 外 国 留学生 到 中 国 后 也 买 自行 车 骑。大
wèi yě mǎi le yíliàng Búguò　tā de zìxíngchē shì jiù de　chángcháng huài　Hǎo
卫 也 买 了 一 辆。不 过，他 的 自行车 是 旧的，常 常 坏。好
zài xiàoyuán lǐ yǒu xiū zìxíngchē de dìfāng　Dàwèi chángcháng qù nàr　xiūchē
在 校 园 里 有 修 自行车 的 地方。大 卫 常 常 去 那儿 修车。
Xiūlǐgōng búdàn dōu hěn yǒu jìshù　érqiě duì rén yě hěn rèqíng
修理工 不但 都 很 有 技术，而且 对 人 也 很 热情。

21.2　词语（Vocabulary）

1. 修理工	xiūlǐgōng	n.	repairman
2. 服务台	fúwùtái	n.	front desk
3. 大灯	dàdēng	n.	main light, ceiling light
4. 坏了	huàile	adj.	broken, having a problem
5. 电工	diàngōng	n.	electrician
6. 师傅	shīfu	n.	master worker
7. 肯定	kěndìng	adv.	certainly
8. 突然	tūrán	adv.	suddenly
9. 灭	miè	v.	to go out (light; fire)
10. 让	ràng	v.	to let, to allow
11. 灯泡	dēngpào	n.	light bulb

12.	开灯	kāidēng	v.	to turn on the light
13.	不用	búyòng	adv.	need not
14.	重要	zhòngyào	adj.	important
15.	工具	gōngjù	n.	instrument, tool
16.	几乎	jīhū	adv.	almost
17.	家家	jiā jiā		every household
18.	连…也…	lián…yě…	expr. pattern	even
19.	辆	liàng	m. w.	measure word for vehicles
20.	不过	búguò	conj.	however, nevertheless
21.	旧	jiù	adj.	old, used
22.	好在	hǎozài	adv.	fortunately
23.	校园	xiàoyuán	n.	campus
24.	有技术	yǒu jìshù	phrase	skillful, well trained
25.	热情	rèqíng	adj.	passionate, warm, enthusiastic

21.3　注释（Notes）

1. 请来修理一下

"一下"用在动词后面表示短暂、不经心的意思，或者表示缓和的语气，功能上与动词重叠相似。

一下 is used after a verb to suggest brevity, casualness, or mildness in tone. It functions very similarly to verb reduplication.

大卫，请你来一下。（David, could you come for a second, please?）
我可以用一下你的笔吗？（May I use your pen for while, please?）

2. 电工师傅

"师傅"在中国大陆一般用来作为对从事体力劳动或服务的人的尊称。1970s—1980s "师傅"曾被用作仅次于"同志"的对陌生人的称呼，现在有一些人觉得"先生"（*Sir*）、"小姐"（*Miss*）太正式，而"同志"有政治色彩时，仍这么使用。

师傅（*master* as opposed to apprentice）is popularly used as a polite form of address to people who work in services on Mainland of China. At one time it was a universal form of address second only to 同志（tóngzhì：comrade）. Today it is still widely used by some people who feel 先生（*Sir*）and 小姐（*Miss*）are too formal and 同志 is too political.

3. 现在都四点了

这里，"都"的意思接近"已经"（*already*），并表明说话者认为"太晚"、"不以为然"。下面是其他例子：

都 is used here to mean *already* and indicates the impatience of the speaker. More examples：

今天都星期五了，你的报告还没写完吗？（It's already Friday today. You still haven't finished writing your report?）

他今年都四十岁了，但是还没有一个女朋友。（He is already 40 this year, but he still doesn't have a girlfriend.）

4. 灯怎么啦？

"怎么啦"用来问"发生了什么事情"、"出了什么问题"。例如：

怎么啦 means *What has happened to it* or *What's wrong with it*. More examples：

你今天怎么啦？不舒服吗？（What has happened to you today? Are you sick?）

你的自行车怎么啦？不能骑了吗？（What is wrong with your bike? Is it broken?）

5. 好在

"好在"强调在不利的情况下的积极、有利的条件或因素，如同英语的 luckily or fortunately：

Just like *luckily* or *fortunately*, 好在 is used to emphasize a positive and favorable element against a negative background：

我不知道她的宿舍在哪儿，也没有她的电话号码，好在我可以给她寄电子邮件，所以还是找到她了。（I didn't know where she lived, nor did I have her phone number. Fortunately, I could send her email messages. Therefore, I managed to find her.）

山本不会说汉语，小王也不会说日文。好在他们都认识汉字，所以还是可以交流。（Yamamoto doesn't speak Chinese and Xiao Wang doesn't speak Japanese. Fortunately they both know characters；therefore，they can still communicate by writing.）

6. 有技术

"有＋N"的形式，有时是形容词。如，

有 can be used with a noun to form 有＋N, some of which are adjectives. For example：

有名（famous）　　　　有钱（rich）
有用（useful）　　　　有趣（interesting）
有利（favorable）　　　有理（reasonable）

有的是形容词短语。如，

Some of the forms are phrases but function as an adjective. For example：

有意思（interesting）　　有技术（skillful）
有能力（capable）　　　　有时间（free，not busy）

21.4　语法（Grammar）

1. 同动词（coverbs）

汉语的"同动词"，部分功能似动词，部分功能似介词，或者说，在意义上它们像动词，而在功能上它们更像介词，所以译成英语就译为介词（*preposition*）。下面是一些例子：

Coverbs in Chinese function partly as verbs and partly as prepositions. They are more like verbs in meaning，but more like prepositions in function. They are often translated into English as prepositions. The following are some examples：

王山每个月都给他父母写信。（Wang Shan writes to his parents every month.）
留学生办公室可以代新来的学生申请居留证。（The International Students' Office can process application for resident ID for newly arrived students.）
请你用圆珠笔填表。（Please fill out the form with a ball-point pen.）
下个星期我要到纽约去。（Next week I'll go to New York.）

老师<u>用</u>中文<u>给</u>三年级的学生上课。（The teacher gives lectures <u>to</u> third-year students <u>in</u> Chinese.）

欧文<u>对</u>中国历史很有兴趣。（Owen is very much interested <u>in</u> Chinese history.）

请大家<u>跟</u>我读课文。（Everybody read <u>after</u> me, please.）

大卫的父母<u>对</u>他的女朋友很热情。（David's parents are very kind and warm <u>to</u> his girlfriend.）

2. 连…都…（even…）

"连…都…"通过指出一种极端的例子表明某种情况的范围。"连"后面的词语在句子中可以担当多种角色。

This is a device used to give an extreme example to show the extent of a situation. The element after 连 can play a variety of grammatical roles in the sentence.

A. 主语（Subject）：

<u>连</u>老师都不认识这个字。（Even the teacher does not know this character.）

<u>连</u>他自己都不知道他有多少钱。（Even he himself doesn't know how much money he has.）

B. 宾语（Object）：

他连<u>课本</u>都没有。（He doesn't even have a textbook.）

他连<u>"一"</u>字都不认识。（He doesn't even know the character *one*.）

C. 时间（Time）：

他爸爸上个月很忙，连<u>星期天</u>都去办公室工作。（His father was very busy last month. He even went to work on Sundays.）

D. 处所（Place）：

这儿的中国饭馆真多，连<u>学校里面</u>都有一家。（There are so many Chinese restaurants here. There is even one inside the school.）

21.5　翻译（Translation）

Lesson Twenty-One　Repair Service

（1）

David：Hello, is this the front desk?

(1)

今天晚上我有一本书要看完，那个电影我们<u>周末再去看</u>，好不好？（I have to finish reading a book tonight. Let's wait until the weekend to see the movie. Is that alright?）

3. 疑问代词用于泛指（QW + 都：Question words used in general reference）

疑问代词与"都"配合，用于泛指（*general reference*），表示"任何"（*any*）的意思，指某类事物中的任何一个事物。

Question words can be used in conjunction with 都 to make a general reference (anything, anybody, any time, anywhere, in any way, etc.).

玛丽的小弟弟才五岁，但是他<u>什么都</u>知道。（Mary's little brother is only five, but he knows everything.）

乔治刚到北京的时候，<u>谁都</u>不认识。（When George had just arrived in Beijing, he didn't know anybody.）

今天下午你<u>什么</u>时候来我<u>都</u>在办公室。（Whenever you come this afternoon, I'll be in my office.）

我这个周末<u>哪儿都</u>不去。（I am not going anywhere this weekend.）

那个歌很难唱，我<u>怎么都</u>学不会。（That song was very hard to sing. I couldn't learn it however hard I tried.）

4. 形容词带程度补语（S Adj 得（S₂）VP）

形容词后面可以带程度补语。程度补语由助词"得"（*de*）加上句子或动词短语构成。形容词后面的程度补语表示形容词所指的性质、属性的程度或引起的结果，作用近于英语的 *it is so adj that...*。

This is a pattern to indicate the extent of a situation by means of a resultant complement, meaning *it is so adj that* ....

昨天我忙<u>得没有时间吃饭</u>。（I was so busy yesterday that I didn't have time to eat.）

他的宿舍冷<u>得我睡不了觉</u>。（His dorm was so cold that I couldn't go to sleep.）

第一次去他女朋友家的时候，大卫紧张<u>得不知道说什么</u>。（When David visited his girlfriend's family for the first time, he was so nervous that he didn't know what to say.）

他们知道了以后，高兴<u>得又唱歌又跳舞</u>。（When they got the news, they were so happy that they started singing and dancing. ）

22.5 翻译（Translation）

Lesson Twenty-Two   Talking about Hobbies and Interests

（1）

David: George, what are you doing?

George: I am writing with a brush, practicing calligraphy.

David: I didn't realize you knew calligraphy.

George: Not yet. I am just learning.

David: Where are you learning it?

George: We have calligraphy and painting workshops at our college. Many foreign students are participating. Why don't you sign up as well?

David: I am busy right now. But I'd like to attend a calligraphy and painting workshop next semester. Where do I sign up though?

George: Room 220 of the Foreign Student Building. By the way, what things do you do for fun?

David: I like to play basketball and go traveling. And I like to dance too.

George: You are interested in so many things. Oh yes, there will be a dance ball tonight in the conference room on the 10th floor. If you want to go, we can go together.

David: Sure.

（2）

It is said that those who don't have any hobbies or interests lead a boring life. Each and every foreign student at our school is interested in something. David likes to play basketball; George likes to play football; Owen is interested in painting and Mary loves dancing. Besides, many of them are also interested in calligraphy and are learning calligraphy with a Chinese teacher.

My hobby is sleeping. With so much going on at school sometimes I don't even have time to eat, much less play ball and paint. So I go to bed whenever I have time.

第二十三课 找书

23.1 课文（Text）

(1)

Dàwèi　Zuótiān wǒ cóng túshūguǎn jiè huílai yì běn shū　xiànzài zhǎo bú dào
大卫：昨 天 我 从 图 书 馆 借 回 来 一 本 书，现 在 找 不 到

le　Nǐ kànjian le ma
了。你 看 见 了 吗？

Ōuwén　Wǒ méi kànjian
欧 文：我 没 看 见。

Dàwèi　Qíguài　wǒ zhǎo le bàntiān le　jiùshì zhǎo bú dào
大卫：奇 怪，我 找 了 半 天 了，就 是 找 不 到。

Ōuwén　Nèi běn shū　nǐ cóng túshūguǎn dài huí sùshè lái le ma
欧文：那 本 书，你 从 图书馆 带 回 宿舍 来 了吗？

Dàwèi　Dài huílai le　Wǒ jì de zuótiān wǒ kāishǐ zuò zuòyè de shíhou　cóng
大卫：带 回来 了。我 记得 昨天 我 开始 做 作业 的 时候，从

shūbāo li ná chūlái fàng zài zhuōzi shàng le
书包 里 拿 出来 放 在 桌子 上 了。

Ōuwén　Zuò wán zuòyè nǐ gàn shénme le
欧文：做 完 作业 你 干 什么 了。

Dàwèi　Zuò wán zuòyè wǒ jiù qù diànnǎoshì tīng lùyīn le
大卫：做 完 作业 我 就 去 电脑室 听 录音 了。

Ōuwén　Nǐ de zuòyè ne
欧文：你的 作业 呢？

Dàwèi　Jīntiān shàngwǔ dài dào xuéxiào qù jiāogěi lǎoshī le
大卫：今天 上午 带 到 学校 去 交给 老师 了。

Ōuwén　Shìbúshì zuòyè hé shū zuótiān yīqǐ fàng jìn nǐ de shūbāo lǐ qù le
欧文：是不是 作业 和 书 昨天 一起 放 进 你的 书包 里 去 了？

Dàwèi　Ràng wǒ kàn kan　　Nǐ shuō duì le　Shū jiù zài shūbāo lǐ
大卫：让 我 看看。……你 说 对 了。书 就 在 书包 里。

Ōuwén　Nǐ zhèi gè rén jiùshì zhèyàng mǎmahūhū de
欧文：你 这 个 人 就是 这 样 马马虎虎 的。

Dàwèi　Wǒ kàn nǐ gēn wǒ yíyàng mǎhu　yǒude shíhou hái bùrú wǒ ne
大卫：我 看 你 跟 我 一样 马虎，有的 时候 还 不如 我 呢。

Ōuwén　Wǒ bāng nǐ zhǎo dào shū le　nǐ búdàn bú xiè wǒ　hái shuō wǒ mǎ
欧文：我 帮 你 找 到 书 了，你 不但 不 谢 我，还 说 我 马

hu bùrú nǐ　Xià cì bù bāng nǐ le
虎、不如 你。下 次 不 帮 你 了。

Dàwèi　Wǒ shì zài gēn nǐ kāi wánxiào　Duōxiè
大卫：我 是 在 跟 你 开 玩笑。多谢。

(2)

Dàwèi de dúshū bàogào jīntiān xiě bù liǎo le　yīnwèi tā cóng túshūguǎn jiè huí
大卫 的 读书 报告 今天 写 不了 了，因为 他 从 图书馆 借回

lái de shū zhǎo bú dào le　Shū hái méiyǒu kàn　zěnme néng xiě dúshū bàogào ne
来 的 书 找 不到 了。书 还 没有 看，怎么 能 写 读书 报告 呢？

Ōuwén cóng wàibiān zǒu jìn sùshè lái de shíhou　Dàwèi wèn Ōuwén kànjian méi kàn
欧文 从 外边 走 进 宿舍 来 的 时候，大卫 问 欧文 看见 没 看

jian tā jiè de shū　Ōuwén wèn Dàwèi nà shì yì běn shénme shū　Dàwèi shuō shì tā
见　他　借　的　书。欧　文　问　大　卫　那　是　一　本　什么　书。大　卫　说　是　他
xiě dúshū bàogào yào yòng de shū　Tā hái shuō jīntiān dúshū bàogào xiě de liǎo xiě
写　读　书　报　告　要　用　的　书。他　还　说　今　天　读　书　报　告　写　得　了　写
bù liǎo quán yào kàn zhǎo de dào zhǎo bú dào nèi běn shū　Tīng le yǐhòu　Ōuwén
不　了　全　要　看　找　得　到　找　不　到　那　本　书。听　了　以后，欧　文
mǎshàng kāishǐ bāngzhù Dàwèi zhǎo shū　yíhuìr jiù zhǎo dào le
马　上　开　始　帮　助　大　卫　找　书，一会儿就　找　到　了。

23.2　词语（Vocabulary）

1. 从	cóng	prep.	from
2. 借	jiè	v.	to borrow
3. 看见	kànjian	v.	to see, to catch sight of
4. 奇怪	qíguài	adj.	odd, strange, weird
5. 记得	jì de	v.	to remember
6. 书包	shūbāo	n.	schoolbag
7. 拿	ná	v.	to take; to hold
8. 放	fàng	v.	to put
9. 听	tīng	v.	to listen to
10. 录音	lùyīn	n.; v.	tape; record
11. 马马虎虎	mǎmahūhū	adj.	careless, inattentive
12. 不如	bùrú	v.	not as good as, inferior to
13. 下次	xià cì		next time
14. 帮	bāng	v.	to help, to assist
15. 跟···开玩笑	gēn···kāi wánxiào	expr. pattern	to kid sb.
16. 多谢	duōxiè	idiomatic expr.	Thanks a lot.
17. 读书报告	dúshū bàogào	n.	reading essay, book review
18. 看	kàn	v.	to depend on
19. 马上	mǎshàng	adv.	immediately, right away
20. 帮助	bāngzhù	v.	to help
21. 一会儿	yíhuìr	n.	a little while

23.3 注释（Notes）

1. 就是找不到

"就是"强调和肯定后面的"找不到"，表示"找不到"是确定无疑的。再如：

In this sentence，就是 means *just*, *simply*, or *no matter how hard it has been tried*, *this is the inevitable result*. Another example：

不知道就是不知道，问也没用。（I just don't know it, it's no use to ask a-gain.）

2. 是不是

肯定句中插入"是不是"可以构成问句。"是不是"通常插入的位置是句子谓语动词前面。

是不是 can be used at different places in a statement to ask a question of confirmation. The typical place for 是不是 is immediately before the verb.

欧文昨天是不是没来？（Owen didn't come yesterday, did he？）

"是不是"也可以插入在句子结尾或开头。如：

It is often used at the beginning or the end of the sentence, too. For example，

我们今天应该交练习，是不是？（We are supposed to hand in the homework today. Is that right？）

是不是一年级的学生都得学汉语？（Is it true that all the first-year students have to learn Chinese？）

3. 马虎，马马虎虎

"马虎"（mǎhu）意思是"不认真"、"不仔细"、"草率"（careless, perfunctory, cursory），"马马虎虎"是"马虎"（mǎhu）的重叠形式。

马虎 means *careless*, *perfunctory*, *cursory*, 马马虎虎 is the duplication of 马虎.

另外，"马马虎虎"可以用来回答"（你）怎么样？"这类的问题，意思是"不好，但是也不是太坏"（so-so）。

马马虎虎 can mean *just so-so* as a response to（你）怎么样？（*How is it going*?）.

4. 下次不帮你了

这里，不 V 了表示 V 以后不进行或不发生。例如：

In this sentence，不 V 了 means *no longer* or *not any more.* More examples：

这条裤子快破了，我以后不穿了。（The trousers are nearly worn-out, I'll wear it no longer. ）

那门课太难。我不学了。（That course is too hard. I quit. ）

他们的那个晚会没有意思，我以后不去了。（Their party is boring. I am not going to it any more. ）

那件事情做完了。下个星期我就不那么忙了。（That job has been completed. Next week I will not be that busy any more. ）

5. 他今天写得了写不了全要看找得到找不到那本书。

"V 得了 V 不了"和"V 得 RC V 不 RC"是可能补语的肯定形式加否定形式构成的正反问句。下面是另外的例子：

V 得了 V 不了, or V 得 RC V 不 RC, is a V－not－V question applied to a potential complement. Other examples：

你明天来得了来不了？（Will you be able, or not able, to come tomorrow?）

这些菜你吃得完吃不完？（Can you, or can you not, finish these dishes?）

"看找得到找不到那本书"意思是"靠找得到找不到那本书决定"，"看"相当于英语的 *depend on*。"全"的意思是"完全"、"全部"，相当于英语的 *totally* 或 *completely*。其他例子如下：

In this sentence，看 in 看找得到找不到那本书 means *depend on*；全 means *totally* or *completely.* More examples：

大卫来不来要看玛丽来不来。（Whether David will come or not depends on

whether Mary comes or not.)

我吃得完吃不完要<u>看</u>这些菜好吃不好吃。(Whether I can finish these dishes depends on whether they are delicious.)

你学得好学不好全要<u>看</u>你花多少时间。(Whether you can learn it well or not totally depends on how much time you spend on it.)

23.4 语法 (Grammar)

1. 趋向补语 (Directional Complement)

涉及移动或方位的动词通常要带上趋向补语指明动词所指的动作、行为与说话人的方向或位置关系。例如,动词"进"(enter) 只有带上趋向补语"来"或"去",成为"进来"(come in) 或"进去"(go in),意思才是完整的。再如,动词"回"(return) 带上趋向补语成为"回来"(come back) 或"回去"(go back),在说"回"的同时,分别说明动作是朝向还是离开说话人的。

Some verbs which involve movement or orientation often need a Directional Complement (来 or 去) to indicate the relative position of the speaker. Therefore, the meaning of *enter* (进), for instance, often does not seem to be complete unless a 来 or 去 is used with it to signal if the movement is toward the speaker (进来: *come in*) or away from the speaker (进去: *go in*). Another example is *return* (回). One often needs to specify whether the subject is moving toward the speaker (回来: *come back*) or away from the speaker (回去: *go back*).

并且,"V + 来/去"这样的组合,还一起作为涉及移动的动词的补语,表明动作的趋向。一个人走进某个地方时,可以是朝向说话人的或者是离开说话人的,分别是"走进来"和"走进去";一个人拿走一件东西,也可以是朝向说话人的或者是离开说话人的,分别是"带回来"和"带回去"。做补语的"V + 来/去"这样的组合被称为"复合趋向补语",如,走<u>进来</u>,拿<u>回去</u>,跑<u>上来</u>,坐<u>下去</u>,等等。

Additionally, combinations like these (V + 来/去) can be used to further complement a movement. A person can *walk into* a place toward or away from the speaker, or *take something back* toward or away from the speaker. These actions are expressed respectively as 走进来, 走进去, and 带回来, 带回去. In such uses, the combined form V + 来/去 (e. g. 走<u>进</u>来, 拿<u>回</u>去, 跑<u>上</u>来, 坐<u>下</u>去) is called a Compound Directional Complement.

还有，如果移动的目的地出现在动词后面，要把它插入在复合趋向补语中间。如，走进<u>教室</u>来（*walk into the classroom*）；带回<u>宿舍</u>去（*take back to the dorm*）。

Furthermore, if the place that the subject is moving into needs to be specified, a place word can be inserted inside the Compound Directional Complement：走进<u>教室</u>来（*walk into the classroom* [where the speaker is]）；带回<u>宿舍</u>去（*take back to the dorm* [away from the speaker]）.

2. A 跟 B 一样 Adj
这个句型用来表示在 Adj 表达的属性上 A 与 B 相同。

This is a pattern used to indicate that two things are the same in a certain respect.

大卫跟乔治一样高。（David is as tall as George.）
这本书跟那本书一样没意思。（This book is as boring as that one.）
学写汉字跟学说话一样重要。（Learning to write characters is as important as learning to speak.）
欧文看中文书跟王山看得一样快。（Owen reads Chinese books as fast as Wang Shan does.）

23.5 翻译（Translation）

Lesson Twenty-Three   Where Is My Book?

（1）

David：I checked out a book yesterday from the library. But now I can't find it anywhere. Did you see it?

George：I didn't.

David：That's weird. I have been looking for it for a long time. It is nowhere to be found.

Owen：Did you bring the book back to the dorm though?

David：Yes, I did. I remember that I took the book out of my bag and put it on the desk when I started to do my homework yesterday.

Owen：What did you do after you were done with your homework?

David: I went to the computer room to listen to the tapes as soon as I was done with my homework.

Owen: Where is your homework?

David: I took it to school this morning and submitted it to the teacher.

Owen: Did you put the book into your bag together with your homework?

David: Let me take a look. You were right. The book is in the bag.

Owen: You are really inattentive!

David: The way I look at it, you are as inattentive as I am. Sometimes, you are even more inattentive than I.

Owen: I helped you find your book. Not only did you not thank me, but you also call me inattentive and said that I was more inattentive than you! I am not going to help you next time.

David: I was just kidding. Thanks a lot.

(2)

David was not able to write his book review today because the book he checked out from the library couldn't be found. Without reading the book, how could he write the review? So when Owen walked into the dorm, David asked him if he saw the book. Owen asked David what kind of book it was. David said that it was the book he needed for writing his review. David said that whether he could write the review depended entirely on whether he could find the book. Upon hearing this, Owen started to help David look for the book right away. It wasn't long before they found it.

第二十四课　选专业

24.1　课文（Text）

（1）

　　王山：大卫，你在美国学什么专业？

　　大卫：我还没有专业。

　　王山：你是大学生，怎么没有专业呢？

　　大卫：在美国，很多大学学生在快学完一年级的时候才选专业。因为我是一

年级的学生，所以还没有选专业呢。

王山：要是你没有专业，你上什么课呢？

大卫：一年级的学生除了上必修的英文写作、外语和数学课以外，想上什么就上什么。

王山：在中国，你考大学的同时就选你想学的专业。考上了的时候就知道你的专业了。

大卫：你们怎么选课呢？

王山：除了少数的选修课以外，大多数的课学校都安排好了。

大卫：要是我学了一年，不喜欢我的专业了，怎么办？可以换专业吗？

王山：换专业比较困难，我想这样的情况比较少。

(2)

　　美国大学生和中国大学生选专业的方法和时间都不一样，但是我认为各有各的好处。美国学生选专业的时间比较晚。在选专业以前先修一些不同的课，看看自己的兴趣在哪里，然后再定专业。这样做的好处是学生可以自我发展，选自己喜欢的专业。只有选自己喜欢的专业才能学得好。这样做不好的地方是进入专业学习比较晚，专业课选得比较少。在中国，学生还没开始上大学就知道自己的专业了。早定专业的好处是进大学以后可以多学专业课，这样可以学得比较多，学得比较深。早定专业不好的地方是学生只学专业课，很少学别的课，学的东西比较窄，还有很多学生开始的时候虽然知道自己的专业，但是并不完全知道自己的专业以后要学什么，要做什么，所以很难说喜欢不喜欢。

24.2　拼音（Pinyin）

(1)

Wáng Shān：Dàwèi, Nǐ zài Měiguó xué shénme zhuānyè?

Dàwèi：Wǒ hái méiyǒu zhuānyè。

Wáng Shān：Nǐ shì dàxuéshēng, zěnme méiyǒu zhuānyè ne?

Dàwèi：Zài Měiguó, hěn duō dàxué xuéshēng zài kuài xué wán yì niánjí de shíhou cái xuǎn zhuānyè。

　　Yīnwèi wǒ shì yì niánjí de xuéshēng, suǒyǐ hái méiyǒu xuǎn zhuānyè ne。

Wáng Shān：Yàoshi nǐ méiyǒu zhuānyè, nǐ shàng shénme kè ne?

Dàwèi：Yì niánjí de xuéshēng chúle shàng bìxiū de yīngwén xiězuò、wàiyǔ hé

shùxué kè yǐwài, xiǎng shàng shénme jiù shàng shénme。

Wáng Shān：Zài Zhōngguó, nǐ kǎo dàxué de tóngshí jiù xuǎn nǐ xiǎng xué de

zhuānyè。Kǎo shàng le de shíhou jiù zhīdào nǐ de zhuānyè le。

Dàwèi：Nǐmen zěnme xuǎn kè ne?

Wáng Shān：Chúle shǎoshù de xuǎnxiūkè yǐwài, dàduōshù de kè xuéxiào dōu

ānpái hǎo le。

Dàwèi：Yàoshi wǒ xué le yì nián, bù xǐhuan wǒ de zhuānyè le, zěnme bàn?

Kěyǐ huàn zhuānyè ma?

Wáng Shān：Huàn zhuānyè bǐjiào kùnnan, wǒ xiǎng zhèyàng de qíngkuàng

bǐjiào shǎo。

（2）

　　Měiguó dàxuéshēng hé Zhōngguó dàxuéshēng xuǎn zhuānyè de fāngfǎ hé shíjiān dōu bù yíyàng, dànshì wǒ rènwéi gè yǒu gè de hǎochu。Měiguó xuéshēng xuǎn zhuānyè de shíjiān bǐjiào wǎn。Zài xuǎn zhuānyè yǐqián xiān xiū yīxiē bùtóng de kè, kànkan zìjǐ de xìngqù zài nǎlǐ, ránhòu zài dìng zhuānyè。Zhèyàng zuò de hǎochu shì xuéshēng kěyǐ zìwǒ fāzhǎn, xuǎn zìjǐ xǐhuan de zhuānyè。Zhǐyǒu xuǎn zìjǐ xǐhuan de zhuānyè cái néng xué de hǎo。Zhèyàng zuò bù hǎo de dìfang shì jìnrù zhuānyè xuéxí bǐjiào wǎn, zhuānyèkè xuǎn de bǐjiào shǎo。Zài Zhōngguó, xuéshēng hái méi kāishǐ shàng dàxué jiù zhīdào zìjǐ de zhuānyè le。Zǎo dìng zhuānyè de hǎochu shì jìn dàxué yǐhòu kěyǐ duō xué zhuānyèkè, zhèyàng kěyǐ xué de bǐjiào duō, xué de bǐjiào shēn。Zǎo dìng zhuānyè bù hǎo de dìfang shì xuéshēng zhǐ xué zhuānyèkè, hěn shǎo xué biéde kè, xué de dōngxi bǐjiào zhǎi, hái yǒu hěn duō xuéshēng kāishǐ de shíhou suīrán zhīdào zìjǐ de zhuānyè, dànshì bìng bù wánquán zhīdào zìjǐ de zhuānyè yǐhòu yào xué shénme, yào zuò shénme, suǒyǐ hěn nán shuō xǐhuan bù xǐhuan。

24.3　词语（Vocabulary）

1. 必修	bìxiū	adj.	required course
2. 写作	xiězuò	n.	writing; composition
3. 外语	wàiyǔ	n.	foreign language
4. 考	kǎo	v.	to take（exams）

5.	少数	shǎoshù	adj.	a few; a small number; minority
6.	选修课	xuǎnxiūkè	n.	elective course
7.	大多数	dàduōshù	n.	most; a large number of; majority
8.	安排	ānpái	v.	to arrange
9.	怎么办	zěnme bàn	v. p.	what can I do?
10.	困难	kùnnan	adj.; n.	difficult
11.	情况	qíngkuàng	n.	situation
12.	方法	fāngfǎ	n.	method; ways and means
13.	认为	rènwéi	v.	to consider, to think
14.	好处	hǎochù	n.	benefit; advantage
15.	修课	xiūkè	v.	to take a class
16.	然后	ránhòu	conj.	then, after that
17.	定	dìng	v.	to decide
18.	自我发展	zìwǒ fāzhǎn	n.	self development
19.	进入	jìnrù	v.	to enter
20.	深	shēn	adj.	deep
21.	并	bìng	adv.	used before a negative for emphasis
22.	完全	wánquán	adj.	completely, absolutely
23.	窄	zhǎi	adj.	narrow

24.4　注释（Notes）

1. 你是大学生怎么没有专业呢？

"怎么"对动作、行为动词发问时，通常是问动作、行为的方式、方法。如：

怎么 can normally mean *how* when used with an action verb, as in

去动物园怎么坐车？（How can I get to the zoo by bus？）

zhuānyè 的 zhuān 怎么写？　（How does one write the character *zhuan*, as in *zhuanye*？）

如果"怎么"后的动词是非动作、行为动词，如"有"、"会"、"知道"，"怎么"问的就是原因、原委。例如：

However, when used with a non-action verb, such as 有, 会, and 知道, 怎么

means *how come* or *why* rather than *how*. For examples：

你<u>怎么</u>有中文名字呢？（How come you have a Chinese name？）

他<u>怎么</u>会说日语？（How come he can speak Japanese？）

你<u>怎么</u>知道她有两个同屋？（How come you know she has two roommates？）

2. 快学完一年级的时候

"快"的意思是时间"接近"、"将近"。下面是又一些例子：

快 here means *almost* or *about to happen*. More examples：

下个星期要交的报告我<u>快</u>写好了。（I am about to finish writing the report that is due next week.）

<u>快</u>毕业的时候，乔治办好了去中国工作的手续。（Shortly before graduation, George completed all the paperwork for going to work in China.）

请你等一下，我<u>快</u>吃完了。（Please wait a second. I am almost done.）

3. 各有各的好处

"各"相当于英语的 *each*，强调不同个体的区别。"各"用作名词的定语，如"各人"（*each person*），"各校"（*each school*），"各国"（*each country*）。"各"修饰的是多音节名词时，名词前面通常要有量词，如"各位老师"，"各个学校"，"各个国家"。

各 means *each*, emphasizing individuality. It can be used as a noun modifier, as in 各人（*each person*），各校（*each school*），and 各国（*each country*）. However, when used before a polysyllabic noun, it usually takes a measure word：各位老师，各个学校，and 各个国家.

每个中文老师都会写汉字，但是<u>各位</u>老师写的汉字不一样。（Every Chinese teacher can write characters, but each teacher writes characters differently.）

每个国家都用钱买东西，但是<u>各国</u>有自己的钱。（Every country uses money for trade, but each country has its own currency.）

"各"也可以作为代词，指已经提到过的一类事物中的不同个体。如"各有各的好处"中的"各"。

各 can also be used as a pronoun, referring to each of a set of things mentioned earlier. In this sentence, 各有各的好处 means *Each has its own merit*.

4. 学生还没开始上大学就知道自己的专业了。

这个句子使用的句型是"S TW 就 V"。这个句子里,"还没开始上大学"是表达时间的短语,"就"用来强调 V 发生的时间早。整个句子的意思是,"学生在上大学前已经知道自己的专业了。"

This sentence follows the S TW 就 V pattern. In this sentence 还没开始上大学 is the time expression, and 就 suggests *earliness*. The whole sentence means *The students knew what their majors would even before coming to the college.*

5. 并不完全知道

副词"并"用在否定句里加强否定的语气,"并"所在句子的意思常常与前面句子的语义趋向相反或相矛盾。例如:

并 is an adverb used in negative sentences to suggest unexpectedness or *contrary to one's assumptions*. For examples:

玛丽的中文说得非常好,但是她并没有去过中国。(Mary speaks very good Chinese. But she has actually never been to China.)

很多人以为汉语很难学,其实汉语的语法并不难。(Many people mistakenly think that Chinese is hard to learn. But in reality, Chinese grammar is not difficult at all.)

大卫并不知道玛丽已经有一个男朋友了。(David doesn't know that, Mary already has a boyfriend.)

24.5 语法(Grammar)

1. 除了…以外…都…

"都"说明所说的事物、人的多数或普遍具有某种性质、属性,"除了…以外"把不具有这种性质、属性的部分排除在外。整个句型与英语的 *all are... except...* 近似。

This pattern is used to exclude certain exceptions from a majority or a general trend, similar to *all are... except...* in English.

除了麻婆豆腐以外，这家饭馆的菜都不好吃。（All the dishes in this restaurant are tasteless except Mrs. Ma's Tofu.）

除了玛丽以外，别的人都去看电影了。（Everyone else has gone to the movie theater except Mary.）

除了一年级的学生以外，别的学生都已经选了专业了。（All the students have decided on their majors except the freshmen.）

乔治除了写毛笔字以外什么爱好都没有。（Except for brush-writing calligraphy, George does not have any hobbies.）

除了这个字以外，这一课里的汉字我都认识。（I know all the characters in this lesson except for this one.）

2. 疑问代词用于任指：想上什么就上什么

疑问代词可以用于"任指"：指某个类或范围里的任何一个。任指的疑问代词相当英语中的 *whatever*，*whoever*，*wherever*，*whenever*，*whichever*，*however* 等。一般来说，疑问代词任指时，句子里有两个相同的疑问代词配合使用。

Question words can be used to make general reference such as *whatever*, *whoever*, *wherever*, *whenever*, *whichever*, *however*, etc. Typically, such a question word correlates with another in the same sentence.

除了必修课以外，<u>什么</u>课有意思我就选<u>什么</u>课。（Apart from the required courses, I'll take whatever course that is interesting.）

<u>谁</u>请他吃饭<u>谁</u>就是他的好朋友。（Whoever invites him to dinner is his good friend.）

如果你有自己的汽车，就可以想去<u>哪儿</u>就去<u>哪儿</u>。（If you have your own car, then you can go wherever you want to go.）

我在宿舍等你，你<u>什么</u>时候来我们就<u>什么</u>时候走。（I'll be waiting for you in the dorm. We'll set off whenever you come.）

在这儿跟在你自己家一样，你想吃<u>什么</u>就吃<u>什么</u>。（Make yourself at home here. Eat whatever you want to eat.）

他爸爸非常喜欢他，他要<u>多少</u>钱他爸爸就给他<u>多少</u>钱。（His father likes him so much that no matter how much money he demands his father always satisfies him.）

24.6 翻译 (Translation)

Lesson Twenty-Four   Choosing a Major

(1)

Wang Shan: David. What is your major in the States?

David: I don't have a major yet.

Wang Shan: You are a college student. How come you don't have a major?

David: Students in American colleges don't have majors until the end of their freshman year. I am still a freshman, so I don't have a major yet.

Wang Shan: How do you decide what courses to take if you don't have a major?

David: There are required courses that freshman students have to take, like English composition, foreign language and math. Then they can take whatever course they like.

Wang Shan: In China, you have to choose your major while you prepare for the college entrance exam. You know what your major is when you are admitted to a college.

David: How do you decide what classes to take?

Wang Shan: Except for a few elective courses, most of the courses that you take are decided by the school administration.

David: What if you decide that you don't like your major after a year in college? Can you change your major?

Wang Shan: Changing your major is rather difficult. I think this only happens rarely.

(2)

The ways and the times in which a major is decided for American students are different from those for Chinese students. But I believe each approach has its own advantages. American students choose their majors at a relatively later stage. The advantage of choosing a major after one has taken a variety of courses to see where one's interest lies is that one can cultivate one's individuality and settle on a major that one truly likes. One can't expect to learn something well unless one's heart is in it. The disadvantage of such an approach, however, is that one gets into an area of study relatively late and one can take fewer courses related to one's major. Chinese students know what their majors are even before they start college. The advantage of having a major early on is that one can take many courses related to one's major once in college. As a result, the students learn about a subject more in depth. The disadvantage of an early decision on a major is that students only take courses related to their major and take very few unrelated courses. As a result, their scope of knowledge is relatively narrow. There are also many students who may know what they want for a major in the beginning, but they don't necessarily have a complete picture as to what they are going to study or do in college. In their case, one's interest isn't really a factor in the choice of a major.

第二十五课　谈汉字

25.1　课文（Text）

（1）（On a bus）

中国人：你好！

大　卫：你好！

中国人：你是美国人吧？

大　卫：你猜对了。

中国人：你的汉语不错，特别是发音很好。

大　卫：谢谢。不过我的声调不行。

中国人：声调确实很难。

大　卫：除了声调，汉字也很难。

中国人：那你能认识多少汉字呢？

大　卫：大概一千多个吧，但只能写几百个。您问的这个问题，只有中国人
　　　　才会问。

中国人：为什么呢？

大　卫：汉语对我们来说是外语，重要的是词，不是字。比方说，"东"是
　　　　一个字，也是一个词，"西"是一个字，也是一个词。"东"和
　　　　"西"两个字在一起，又是一个新的词"东西"。

中国人：你说得很有道理。这一点我以前没有注意到。看来中国人学汉语和
　　　　外国人学汉语就是不一样。

(2)

　　我觉得学汉语写字最难。有些字笔画很多，很难记，有些字看起来差不多，
很容易写错，所以我每天都花很多时间练习写汉字。有的人说，现在电脑这么发
达，打拼音，汉字就会出来，为什么还要用手写呢？要是只认字，不记每个字怎
么写，这样就可以省很多时间。我觉得记汉字、写汉字，难是难，但是汉字是中
国文化的一部分，只有一笔一画地写才能真正了解汉语和中国文化。

25.2　拼音（Pinyin）

(1)

Zhōngguórén：Nǐ hǎo！

Dàwèi：Nǐ hǎo！

Zhōngguórén：Nǐ shì Měiguórén ba？

Dàwèi：Nǐ cāi duì le。

Zhōngguórén：Nǐ de Hànyǔ búcuò，tèbié shì fāyīn hěn hǎo。

Dàwèi：Xièxie。Búguò wǒ de shēngdiào bùxíng。

Zhōngguórén：Shēngdiào quèshí hěn nán。

Dàwèi：Chúle shēngdiào，hànzì yě hěn nán。

Zhōngguórén：Nà nǐ néng rènshi duōshǎo hànzì ne？

Dàwèi：Dàgài yì qiān duō gè ba，dàn zhǐnéng xiě jǐ bǎi gè。Nín wèn de zhè gè
　　　　wèntí，zhǐyǒu Zhōngguórén cái huì wèn。

Zhōngguórén：Wèishénme ne？

Dàwèi：Hànyǔ duì wǒmen lái shuō shì wàiyǔ，zhòngyào de shì cí，bú shì zì。

Bǐfang shuō, "dōng" shì yí gè zì, yě shì yí gè cí, "xī" shì yí gè zì, yě shì yí gè cí。 "dōng" hé "xī" liǎng gè zì zài yīqǐ, yòu shì yí gè xīn de cí "dōngxi"。

Zhōngguórén: Nǐ shuō de hěn yǒu dàolǐ。 Zhèi yì diǎn wǒ yǐqián méiyǒu zhùyì dào。 Kànlái Zhōngguórén xué Hànyǔ hé wàiguórén xué Hànyǔ jiùshì bù yīyàng!

(2)

Wǒ juéde xué Hànyǔ xiě zì zuì nán。 Yǒuxiē zì bǐhuà hěn duō, hěn nán jì, yǒuxiē zì kàn qǐlái chàbuduō, hěn róngyì xiě cuò, suǒyǐ wǒ měi tiān dōu huā hěn duō shíjiān liànxí xiě hànzì。 Yǒu de rén shuō xiànzài diànnǎo zhème fādá, dǎ pīnyīn, hànzì jiù huì chūlái, wèishénme hái yào yòng shǒu xiě ne? Yàoshi zhǐ rèn zì, bú jì měi gè zì zěnme xiě, zhèyàng jiù kěyǐ shěng hěnduō shíjiān。 Wǒ juéde jì hànzì、 xiě hànzì, nán shì nán, dànshì hànzì shì Zhōngguó wénhuà de yí bùfen, zhǐyǒu yìbǐyíhuà de xiě cáinéng zhēnzhèng liǎojiě Hànyǔ hé Zhōngguó wénhuà。

25.3　词语（Vocabulary）

1. 猜	cāi	v.	to guess
2. 特别	tèbié	adv.	specially
3. 发音	fāyīn	n.	pronunciation
4. 声调	shēngdiào	n.	tone
5. 不行	bùxíng	adj.	not good (Lit. cannot pass)
6. 确实	quèshí	adv.	indeed
7. 大概	dàgài	adv.	probably, approximately
8. 千	qiān	num.	thousand
9. 问题	wèntí	n.	question
10. 为什么	wèishénme	inter. pron.	why
11. 词	cí	n.	word
12. 比方说	bǐfang shuō	phrase	for example
13. 有道理	yǒu dàolǐ	phrase	reasonable, right
14. 注意	zhùyì	v.	to pay attention to; to be aware of
15. 看来	kànlái	v.	it seems, it looks

16.	笔画	bǐhuà	n.	strokes
17.	记	jì	v.	to remember
18.	容易	róngyì	adj.	easy; easily
19.	花时间	huā shíjiān	phrase	time consuming
20.	拼音	pīnyīn	n.	Pinyin; spelling
21.	省	shěng	v.	to save
22.	文化	wénhuà	n.	culture
23.	部分	bùfen	n.	part
24.	一笔一画	yìbǐyíhuà	phrase	stroke by stroke
25.	真正	zhēnzhèng	adj.	really; indeed

25.4 注释（Notes）

1. 特别

"特别"修饰形容词或心理动词时，说明程度深，意思是"格外"、"不一般"。如：

特别 can be used with an adjective or mental verb to mean *especially* or *extremely*, such as：

这个字笔画<u>特别</u>多，<u>特别</u>容易写错。（This character has quite a lot of strokes and it is very easy to write it wrong.）

他<u>特别</u>喜欢吃辣的。（He loves to eat peppery stuff.）

"特别"修饰"是"引出的名词或小句时，作用是从同类事物中指出不一般的一项进一步加以说明：

When 特别 is followed by a noun or a clause, it needs to be introduced by 是：

他家的孩子学习都非常好，<u>特别是</u>他弟弟。（The children in his family are all good students, especially his younger brother.）

这个学校的东亚系很好，<u>特别是</u>他们的中国历史研究是美国最好的。（The department of East Asian studies in this university is very good. In particular, their Chinese history studies is the best in the US.）

2. 那你能认识多少汉字呢？

这里"那"是连词，表示在前面的话的基础上做出的推理。再如：

In this sentence, 那 serves as a connective device, meaning *in that case*.... Another example：

你说你认识她，那她叫什么？ （You said you know her, then, what is her name?）

3. 汉语对我们来说是外语，重要的是词，不是字

"对…来说"引出看待事物的主体。表示从"我们"的角度看，"汉语是外语，重要的是词，不是字"。

This idiomatic phrase means *to us*... or *as far as we are concerned*...：

写汉字对日本学生来说不是难事，但是对美国学生来说是很费时间的事。（To Japanese students, writing characters is no big deal. But to American students, it is very time-consuming. ）

对很多北京人来说，上海话就像是外国话。（To many Beijing people, Shanghai dialect is like a foreign language. ）

对一年级的学生来说，每一门课都跟专业课一样重要。（To first-year students, every course is as important as their major courses. ）

4. 看来

"看来"表示依据已知的情况进行估计、猜测，作为插入语，多放在句子开头：

看来 means *it looks as if / though*..., and it is usually used as a parentheses：

看来汉语不是那么难学。（It looks as though Chinese is not all that difficult to learn. ）

看来乔治九点半以前来不了。（It looks as though George won't able to come before 9:30. ）

看来你得换一个专业。（It looks as if you need to change your major. ）

5. 中国人学汉语和外国人学汉语就是不一样

"就是"在这里用来加强判断的语气，表示对做出的判断充分肯定。

In this sentence，就是 suggests a reaffirmed belief，comparable in tone to *indeed* in English.

25.5　语法（Grammar）

A 是 A，但是…

"A 是 A"相当于"虽然 A"，对 A 先加以肯定，在"但是"后面提出与 A 的语义趋向不同的内容。这个句型多用来委婉地表示不同别人的看法。

This pattern is used to acknowledge a foregoing point and then present a different opinion. It is typically used to express polite disagreement.

那个大学有名是有名，但是学费太贵。（That university is indeed famous，but its tuition is very expensive.）

坐地铁便宜是便宜，但是有些地方坐地铁去不了。（It is true that taking the subway is cheaper，but there are places the subway doesn't go.）

我的宿舍小是小，但是离学校不远，很方便。（It is true that my dorm is small，but it is close to the school and very convenient.）

25.6　翻译（Translation）

Lesson Twenty-Five　Talking about Chinese Characters

（1）（On a bus）

Chinese：Hello！

David：Hi！

Chinese：You are American，right？

David：You're right.

Chinese：Your Chinese is pretty good. Your pronunciation is especially good.

David：Thanks. But my tones aren't that good.

Chinese：Tones are difficult.

David：Besides tones，characters are hard too.

Chinese：How many characters do you know now？

David：Probably over a thousand. But I can only write a few hundred. This is a question only a Chinese person asks.

Chinese: How so?

David: To people like me, Chinese is a foreign language where what matters is words, not characters. For example, *dong* is a character as well as a word; so is *xi*. But when you put them together, *dongxi* becomes a new word.

Chinese: You made a good point. I didn't notice that before. Evidently there is a difference between the way the Chinese learn the Chinese language and the way foreigners learn it.

(2)

I think writing characters is the most difficult part of learning Chinese. Some characters have so many strokes that it is very hard for one to memorize them. There are also characters that look so much alike that it is easy to make a mistake. This is why I spend a lot of time every day practicing characters. Some people raise the question: with computers so prevalent, what is the point of writing characters by hand when you can get the characters simply by typing in the Pinyin on the keyboard? You can save yourself a lot of time if you just focus on recognizing characters and not on memorizing how to write them. However, I believe characters are a component of the Chinese culture. Although they are difficult to remember and to write, you have to learn them stroke by stroke to achieve a true understanding of the Chinese language and the Chinese culture.

第二十六课　做客

26.1　课文（Text）

(1)

李老师夫人：外面刮着风，下着雨，大卫他们会来吗？
李老师：我们约好的，他们一定会来的。

（敲门的声音）

李夫人：他们来了。
李老师：（开开门）欢迎！欢迎！

李夫人：请坐，请喝茶。

大卫、南西：谢谢！（坐下）

李夫人：这么大的雨，你们怎么来的？

大　卫：坐出租车来的。我们带着雨伞呢。

南　西：你们的房子又大又亮，真不错。

李夫人：这房子是新盖的。

大　卫：你们的孩子呢？

李夫人：孩子在外地上学。

李老师：今天你们尝尝我爱人做的家常菜。

大卫、南西：太好了，我们早就想吃了。

李老师：都准备好了。

大　卫：好香啊！

李老师：别急，你们休息休息，然后吃饭。

（2）

前不久，我和欧文去一位中国朋友的家里做客。他家离我们学校不远，大约有五十公里。他家人都很热情、好客。那天，他母亲做了十多个菜，摆满了一桌子。我们吃着女主人亲手做的饭菜，又说又笑，开心极了。他们还不停地用筷子给我们夹菜。以前我就听说这是中国人招待客人的习惯，这次我们有了亲身体会。

26.2　拼音（Pinyin）

（1）

Lǐ lǎoshī fūrén：Wàimiàn guā zhe fēng，xià zhe yǔ，Dàwèi tāmen huì lái ma？

Lǐ lǎoshī：Wǒmen yuē hǎo de，tāmen yídìng huì lái de。

Lǐ fūrén：Tāmen lái le。

Lǐ lǎoshī：Huānyíng！huānyíng！

Lǐ fūrén：Qǐng zuò，qǐng hē chá。

Dàwèi、Nánxī：Xièxie！

Lǐ fūrén：Zhème dà de yǔ，nǐmen zěnme lái de？

Dàwèi：Zuò chūzūchē lái de。Wǒmen dài zhe yǔsǎn ne。

Nánxī：Nǐmen de fángzi yòu dà yòu liàng，zhēn búcuò。

Lǐ fūrén：Zhèi fángzi shì xīn gài de。

Dàwèi：Nǐmen de háizi ne?

Lǐ fūrén：Háizi zài wàidì shàngxué。

Lǐ lǎoshī：Jīntiān nǐmen cháng cháng wǒ àiren zuò de jiāchángcài。

Dàwèi、Nánxī：Tài hǎo le，wǒmen zǎojiù xiǎng chī le。

Lǐ lǎoshī：Dōu zhǔnbèi hǎo le。

Dàwèi：Hǎo xiāng a!

Lǐ lǎoshī：Bié jí，nǐmen xiūxi xiūxi，ránhòu chīfàn。

（2）

　　Qiánbùjiǔ，wǒ hé Ōuwén qù yí wèi Zhōngguó péngyou de jiālǐ zuòkè。Tā jiā lí wǒmen xuéxiào bù yuǎn，dàyuē yǒu 50 gōnglǐ。Tā jiā rén dōu hěn rèqíng、hàokè。Nèi tiān，tā mǔqīn zuò le shí duō gè cài，bǎi mǎn le yì zhuōzi。Wǒmen chī zhe nǚzhǔrén qīnshǒu zuò de fàncài，yòu shuō yòu xiào，kāixīn jí le。Tāmen hái bùtíng de yòng kuàizi gěi wǒmen jiā cài。Yǐqián wǒ jiù tīngshuō zhè shì Zhōngguórén zhāodài kèrén de xíguàn，zhèi cì wǒmen yǒu le qīnshēn tǐhuì。

26.3　词语（Vocabulary）

1. 做客	zuòkè	v.	to be a guest
2. 夫人	fūrén	n.	madam, Mrs.
3. 着	zhe	particle	used after a verb to indicate continuation
4. 约好	yuē hǎo	v.	to arrange；to agree on a time or place（to meet）
5. 茶	chá	n.	tea
6. 雨伞	yǔsǎn	n.	umbrella
7. 房子	fángzi	n.	house
8. 盖	gài	v.	to build
9. 孩子	háizi	n.	children；child
10. 外地	wàidì	n.	other places
11. 尝	cháng	v.	to taste；to try the taste
12. 爱人	àiren	n.	spouse；lover
13. 家常菜	jiāchángcài	n.	homemade dishes
14. 别	bié	adv.	don't

15.	急	jí	adj.	impatient, irritated, worrying
16.	前不久	qián bùjiǔ	phrase	not long ago
17.	大约	dàyuē	adv.	approximately
18.	公里	gōnglǐ	n.	kilometer
19.	好客	hàokè	v.	hospitable
20.	母亲	mǔqin	n.	mother
21.	摆	bǎi	v.	to put, to place
22.	满	mǎn	adj.	full, filled, packed
23.	女主人	nǚzhǔrén	n.	hostess
24.	亲手	qīnshǒu	adv.	(do/make) personally
25.	笑	xiào	v.	to smile, to laugh
26.	开心	kāixīn	adj.	happy; rejoice
27.	极了	jí le		extremely (used after an adj.)
28.	不停地	bùtíng de	adv.	non-stop, incessantly
29.	筷子	kuàizi	n.	chopsticks
30.	夹菜	jiācài	v.	to pick up food with chopsticks
31.	听说	tīngshuō	v.	heard about
32.	招待	zhāodài	v.	to host
33.	客人	kèrén	n.	guest
34.	亲身	qīnshēn	adv.	by oneself, personally (experience)
35.	体会	tǐhuì	v.	to experience; to realize

26.4　注释（Notes）

1. 他们是一定会来的

语型"是…的"的一个用法是用来表示"确信"。使用"是…的"的句子不是叙述事件或事情的情况，而是表明说话人的看法和态度。下面是其他的例子：

Another use of the "是…的" construction is to present a belief or conviction. The function of a sentence framed in this structure is not to narrate an event or describe a situation, but rather to express the speaker's opinion or attitude. The following are more examples：

你做的好事大家<u>是</u>不会忘记<u>的</u>。(I can assure you that the good things you did will not be forgotten by people.)

一个学期同时选六门课而且都学得很好是不可能的。（I don't think it is possible to take six courses in one semester and do all of them well. ）

现在是上下班时间，那条路是一定会堵车的。（It is rush hour now, and there surely will be traffic jams on that road. ）

2. 爱人

在中国大陆，"爱人"是个中性的称呼：男人说的时候指妻子，女人说的时候指丈夫。而在中国的台湾、香港，"爱人"的意思是"情人"。所以，在中国大陆，听到有人说"你爱人叫你早点儿回去"是很自然的事情，而在中国的台湾、香港，这样的话是会令人尴尬的。

On mainland of China, 爱人, meaning *spouse*, is a neutral form of address which indicates wife when said by a man and husband by a woman, whereas in Taiwan and Hong Kong of China it means *lover*. Therefore, it is perfectly natural to hear somebody say "你爱人叫你早点儿回去" （Your wife/husband called to ask you to go home earlier today.) on mainland of China, while such a sentence would sound very awkward in Taiwan and Hong Kong of China.

3. 我们早就想吃了

这是用句型 S TW 就 V 构成的句子，"早"用作时间词（TM）表示"很早以前"的意思。这种句子里，"早"如果读得较重，常常伴有"不耐烦"、"担心"、"自以为是"等意味。

This sentence fits the pattern S TW 就 V, with 早 functioning as the TW. What needs to be pointed out is that a sentence involving 早就 in this way often carries an attitude, such as impatience, anxiety, or even arrogance.

我早就知道了。（I knew it long time ago. ［I don't need you to tell me now. ］）

我们早就想学用字典了。（We have long wanted to learn how to use a dictionary. ）

她早就选好专业了。（She decided her major a long time ago. ）

大卫早就毕业了。（David graduated a long time ago. ［You didn't know that?］）

4. 十多个菜

"十多"表示一个介于 10 和 20 之间的概数，一般不会超过 15，"二十多"与之相似。同样，"一百多"表示比 100 多但一般不会超过 150 的概数，"三千多"表示比3 000多但一般不会超过3 500的概数。

十多 expresses an approximate number more than 10 and less than 20, most probably from 11 to 15. 二十多 is similar. 一百多 is more than 100 less probably than 150；and 三千多 is more than 3,000 and less probably than 3,500.

5. 开心极了

"极"本来的意思是"尽头"（Adj 极了），"极了"有"到了尽头"的意思，用在形容词后做补语，表示对程度的强化或夸张。"极"作为一个程度副词也可以用在形容词前面，语意比"很"、"非常"、"特别"重。

极 literally means *extreme* and functions similarly to an intensifier when used after an adjective（Adj 极了）. It is stronger in tone than other intensifiers such as 很, 非常, and 特别.

那个自由市场上卖的水果便宜极了。(The fruits sold on that free market were extremely cheap.)

她做的菜好吃极了。(The dishes she cooked were extremely delicious.)

乔治的女朋友唱歌唱得好极了。(George's girlfriend is an extremely good singer.)

这个市场的菜极便宜。(The vegetables in this market are extremely cheap.)

26.5　语法（Grammar）

V 着

"着"（*zhe*）是表明动词持续状态的助词。虽然句子的"V 着"常常译成英语的进行体（*to be doing*），但是它与"在 V"不同：后者表示动作行为在进行中，而前者表示状态的持续。例如：

着 is a verb particle indicating a continuous state. Although such V 着 in a sentence is often translated into English as *to be doing*, it differs from 在 V：while the latter signals the progress of an action, the former indicates the continuation of a state. More examples：

大卫看<u>着</u>玛丽。（David is staring at Mary.）

玛丽拿<u>着</u>一本书。（Mary is holding a book in her hand.）

这个老师喜欢坐<u>着</u>上课。（This teacher likes to give lectures while sitting.）

乔治喜欢唱<u>着</u>歌开车。（George likes to sing while driving.）

26.6 翻译（Translation）

Lesson Twenty-Six   Being a Guest

（1）

Teacher Li's Wife：Do you think David and others will make it when it is this windy and rainy outside?

Teacher Li：We have an appointment. So they will come for sure.

（Knocks on the door）

Mrs. Li：Here they are.

Teacher Li：(opens the door) Welcome.

Mrs. Li：Take a seat please. And have some tea.

David and Nancy ：Thanks. (They sit down)

Mrs. Li：How did you get here with the rain this nasty?

David：We got a cab. And we have our umbrellas.

Nancy：Such a big house and so bright. It is wonderful!

Mrs. Li：It was built not long ago.

David：Where are your children?

Mrs. Li：They are attending schools in other cities.

Teacher Li：You will have a taste of my wife's home cooking today.

David and Nancy：Great! We have long been looking forward to it.

Teacher Li：The food is ready.

David：It smells so good.

Teacher Li：No hurry. You can catch your breath and then we will eat.

（2）

A few days ago, Owen and I were invited by a Chinese friend to visit him. His home is not far from our school—about 50 kilometers. Everybody in his family was warm and friendly. His mother cooked more than ten dishes on that day. The dining table was covered with food. We chatted and laughed while we enjoyed the dishes cooked especially for us by the hostess of the house. We had a great time. Our hosts constantly put food onto our plates too. We had heard about the Chinese customs in entertaining a guest, but it wasn't until that visit that we actually experienced them.

第二十七课　看大夫

27.1　课文（Text）

（1）我有点儿不舒服

（六点过一点儿，大卫走进乔治的房间，乔治在床上躺着）

大卫：乔治，你怎么还在睡觉？该起来了。吃晚饭了！
乔治：我有点儿不舒服，头疼、发烧，全身没有力气。
大卫：你可能是感冒了。我陪你去医院看看吧。
乔治：不用了，我已经吃药了。

大卫：量一下体温吧。

（乔治量体温。几分钟以后……）

大卫：多少度？

乔治：四十度。

大卫：太高了。咱们最好去医院请大夫看看。

乔治：现在医院已经下班了吧？

大卫：医院有急诊室，二十四小时都有人。

乔治：那好吧。

大卫：你想不想先吃点儿东西？这儿有牛奶和饼干。

乔治：我一点儿胃口也没有。

大卫：那咱们现在就走吧。

乔治：等一等，我带点儿零钱。

大卫：对了，把证件带上。

(2) 是不是黄瓜没洗干净

吃完午饭，小高觉得肚子有点儿疼。他上了一趟厕所，发现自己拉肚子了。他吃了一些药，可是，肚子越来越疼。他只好去医院看病。大夫问了他的病情后，给他开了药方，跟他说一定要按时吃药。大夫还说，以后吃东西一定要注意卫生。听了大夫的话，小高才想起来，自己中午吃了生黄瓜，可能是黄瓜没有洗干净。自己做事总是马马虎虎的，以后一定要注意。

27.2 拼音（Pinyin）

(1) Wǒ yǒudiǎnr bù shūfu

Dàwèi：Qiáozhì, nǐ zěnme hái zài shuìjiào? Gāi qǐlái le。Chī wǎnfàn le!

Qiáozhì：Wǒ yǒudiǎnr bù shūfu, tóuténg、fāshāo, quánshēn méiyǒu lìqi。

Dàwèi：Nǐ kěnéng shì gǎnmào le。Wǒ péi nǐ qù yīyuàn kàn kan ba。

Qiáozhì：Bú yòng le, wǒ yǐjīng chī yào le。

Dàwèi：Liáng yíxià tǐwēn ba。

Dàwèi：Duōshǎo dù?

Qiáozhì：Sìshí dù。

Dàwèi：Tài gāo le。Zánmen zuìhǎo qù yīyuàn qǐng dàifu kàn kan。

Qiáozhì：Xiànzài yīyuàn yǐjīng xiàbān le ba?

Dàwèi：Yīyuàn yǒu jízhěnshì，èrshísì xiǎoshí dōu yǒurén。

Qiáozhì：Nà hǎo ba。

Dàwèi：Nǐ xiǎng bù xiǎng xiān chī diǎnr dōngxi? Zhèr yǒu niúnǎi hé bǐnggān。

Qiáozhì：Wǒ yīdiǎnr wèikǒu yě méiyǒu。

Dàwèi：Nà zánmen xiànzài jiù zǒu ba。

Qiáozhì：Děng yì děng，wǒ dài diǎnr língqián。

Dàwèi：Duì le，bǎ zhèngjiàn dài shang。

（2）Shìbúshì huánggua méi xǐ gānjìng

Chī wán wǔfàn，Xiǎo Gāo juéde dùzi yǒu diǎnr téng。Tā shàng le yí tàng cèsuǒ，fāxiàn zìjǐ lādùzi le。Tā chī le yīxiē yào，kěshì，dùzi yuèláiyuè téng。Tā zhǐhǎo qù yīyuàn kànbìng。Dàifu wèn le tā de bìngqíng hòu，gěi tā kāi le yàofāng，gēn tā shuō yídìng yào ànshí chī yào。Dàifu hái shuō，yǐhòu chī dōngxi yídìng yào zhùyì wèishēng。Tīng le dàifu de huà，Xiǎo Gāo cái xiǎng qǐlái，zìjǐ zhōngwǔ chī le shēng huánggua，kěnéng shì huánggua méiyǒu xǐ gānjìng。Zìjǐ zuòshì zǒngshì mǎmahūhū de，yǐhòu yídìng yào zhùyì。

27.3　词语（Vocabulary）

1. 头疼	tóuténg	v.	to have a headache
2. 发烧	fāshāo	v.	to have a fever
3. 全身	quánshēn	n.	entire body
4. 力气	lìqi	n.	strength，energy
5. 感冒	gǎnmào	v.	to get a cold
6. 医院	yīyuàn	n.	hospital
7. 药	yào	n.	medicine
8. 量	liáng	v.	to measure
9. 体温	tǐwēn	n.	body temperature
10. 最好	zuìhǎo	adv.	had better
11. 大夫	dàifu	n.	doctor（medical）
12. 急诊室	jízhěnshì	n.	emergency room

13. 牛奶	niúnǎi	n.	milk
14. 饼干	bǐnggān	n.	cookie
15. 胃口	wèikou	n.	appetite
16. 零钱	língqián	n.	change; coins, small bills
17. 证件	zhèngjiàn	n.	identification card or paper
18. 黄瓜	huánggua	n.	cucumber
19. 洗	xǐ	v.	to wash
20. 肚子	dùzi	n.	abdomen
21. 趟	tàng	m. w.	measure word for trips
22. 发现	fāxiàn	v.	to discover, to find
23. 拉肚子	lā dùzi	v.	to have loose bowels
24. 越来越	yuèláiyuè	idiom. phrase	even more
25. 看病	kànbìng	v.	to see a doctor
26. 病情	bìngqíng	n.	state of an illness
27. 开药方	kāi yàofāng	v.	to prescribe medicine
28. 按时	ànshí	adv.	on schedule
29. 卫生	wèishēng	n.	health, hygiene, sanitation
30. 生	shēng	adj.	raw; uncooked
31. 总是	zǒngshì	adv.	always

27.4 注释（Notes）

1. 该起来了

"该"在这里的意思同"应该"，"该 V 了"表示"从时间上看应该 V 了"，相当于英语的 *It's time to . . .*。

该 is a short form for 应该. 该 V 了 is a pattern used to say *It's time to . . . .*

该上课了。(It's time to go to / start class.)
该吃饭了。(It's time to eat.)
该睡觉了。(It's time to go to bed.)

2. 我想吃点东西

"想"在这里的意思是"希望"、"打算"，它与"要"的不同是：1）"要"

表示的"需要"、"希望"更强烈；2）"想"可以受程度副词的修饰，而"要"不可以：

想 here means *to intend* or *to want*. It is different from 要 in that 1）要 expresses a stronger desire or wish；and 2）想 can be modified by an intensifier whereas 要 cannot be so modified：

我<u>很</u>想学写毛笔字。(I am very much interested to learn to write with a writing brush.)

大卫<u>非常</u>想跟玛丽一起去北京旅游。(David would very much like to go with Mary on a tour to Beijing.)

3. 对了

"对了"作为插入语，表示突然"想起了什么事情"或者"旧话题中断后突然想起新的话题"。

This expression is often used when one wants to express something that suddenly comes to mind, or to start an unrelated topic, equivalent in English to *Oh yes...*, *Before I forget...*, and *By the way....*

4. 想起来

"起来"本来的意思是"从低到高、从下到上"。这里，与"想"一起使用做补语，表示"想"有了结果、达到目的。"想不起来"则表示"想了可没有结果"。

起来 literally means *to get up* or *to rise*. When used with 想 as it is here, it means *to evoke* or *to bring up*. The whole phrase, 想起来, means *to recall* or *to remember*.

我想起来了，我是三年前在上海见到他的。(Now I remember, I met him in Shanghai three years ago.)

我认识她，但是她的名字我现在<u>想不起来</u>了。(I know her, but I can't recall what her name is now.)

5. 只好

"只好"表示"没有其他的选择，只能/只有……"。

只好 means *cannot but. . .* or *out of choices, one has to. . . .*

他的钱用完了，<u>只好</u>给他爸爸写信。(He was out of money and had to write to his father.)

我今天头疼、发烧，全身没有力气，<u>只好</u>在家休息，不去上课了。(I have a headache and a fever. My entire body feels weak. I can't do anything but rest at home today instead of going to class.)

27.5 语法（Grammar）

1. S 一点儿（O）也不/没有 V

这个句型表示全部的、彻底的否定。其中，"也"可以换用"都"。例如：

This is a pattern used to express whole and entire negation. 都 can be used in place of 也. For example：

我<u>一点儿也不</u>喜欢打球。(I don't like to play ball at all.)

他对数学<u>一点兴趣也没有</u>。(He doesn't have any interest in mathematics.)

我这个学期上的选修课<u>一点也不</u>难。(The elective courses I am taking this semester are not difficult at all.)

2. 上了一趟厕所

"趟"在这个句子里是动量词，用来表示动作、行为进行的次数。动量词还有"次"、"回"、"遍"等。

In this sentence, 趟 acts as a measure word used after a verb to indicate the number of *rounds* or *times* an action is carried out. Other verbal measure words include 次, 回, and 遍, etc..

上个星期我去了两<u>趟</u>纽约。(Last week I went to New York twice.)

那个电影我看了三<u>次</u>。(I have seen that movie three times.)

昨天我去了两<u>回</u>图书馆，还去了一<u>回</u>老师的办公室。(Yesterday I went to the library twice, and I went to the teacher's office once.)

这一课的汉字我写了七<u>遍</u>。(I wrote the characters in this lesson seven times.)

3. 越来越…

"越来越"用在形容词或"喜欢"、"恨"之类表示心理活动或状态的动词前面，表示它们所指性质、状态的程度随着时间的推移或相关动作行为的发展而加深。与英语的"*more and more*"意思相仿。

This phrase is used before an adjective or a verb such as *like* or *hate* to express increasing intensity, equivalent to *more and more* in English.

春天到了，天气<u>越来越</u>好了。(The spring is coming. The weather is getting better and better.)

我们认识的汉字<u>越来越</u>多了。(We can recognize more and more characters.)

欧文每天都练习写汉字，他现在写得<u>越来越</u>好看了。(Owen keeps practicing writing characters every day. Now he writes characters increasingly better.)

用豆腐做菜的方法真多，我<u>越来越</u>喜欢吃豆腐了。(There are so many ways to cook tofu, I have come increasingly to like to eat tofu.)

27.6　翻译（Translation）

Lesson Twenty-Seven　Seeing a Doctor

（1）I Am Sick.

(A few minutes past 6, David walks into George's room. George is lying in bed.)

David：George, how come you are still in bed? Get up. It's dinner-time!
George：I am sick. I have a headache and a temperature. And I feel exhausted.
David：You probably got a cold. Let me go to the hospital with you.
George：No, thanks. I took some pills.
David：Let me take your temperature.

(George takes the thermometer. A few minutes later...)

David：What's the temperature?
George：Forty degrees.

David：That is really high. We'd better go the hospital to see a doctor.

George：The hospital must be closed by now.

David：But there is an emergency room in the hospital. There are people on duty around the clock.

George：All right.

David：Would you like to eat something first? You have milk and some crackers.

George：I don't have any appetite.

David：Let's go then.

George：Wait a minute. Let's me take some money.

David：Oh yes. And bring your ID with you too.

（2）Was It Because the Cucumber Wasn't Well Cleaned?

Xiao Gao had a stomachache after lunch. He went to the bathroom and realized that he had diarrhea. He took some medicine, but the pain grew worse. He had no choice but to go to the hospital. The doctor wrote him a prescription after asking him some questions and told him to take the medication on time. The doctor also told him that he should be careful about what he eats. Upon hearing this, Xiao Gao remembered that he had some uncooked cucumber for lunch. It might be that the cucumber wasn't clean enough. He knew that he was often too careless, so he decided to be careful from now on.

第二十八课　收拾宿舍

28.1　课文（Text）

(1)

乔治：咱们的宿舍这么乱，什么东西也找不到。

大卫：对，桌上、地上都是书，衣服哪儿都是。要是带朋友来，连坐的地方都没有。

乔治：真应该收拾收拾了。

大卫：你说得很对。现在就开始吧。

乔治：我们先把自己的书收拾好，你擦桌子，我扫地，把要洗的衣服放在一起。收拾完屋子，我们一起去洗衣服。

（2）

从搬进来的那天起，大卫和他的同屋乔治从来没有收拾过他们的宿舍。桌子上放满了书。衣服、鞋和袜子扔得满地都是。今天大卫和乔治决定一起收拾屋子。他们先把书放回书架上去，再把衣服从地上捡起来，把干净的放进衣柜里，把脏的放在一起，准备去洗。他们很快就把房间收拾干净了。

28.2 拼音（Pinyin）

（1）

Qiáozhì：Zánmen de sùshè zhème luàn, shénme dōngxi yě zhǎo bú dào。

Dàwèi：Duì, zhuō shàng、dìshàng dōu shì shū, yīfu nǎr dōu shì。Yàoshi dài péngyou lái, lián zuò de dìfang dōu méiyǒu。

Qiáozhì：Zhēn yīnggāi shōushi shōushi le。

Dàwèi：Nǐ shuō de hěn duì。Xiànzài jiù kāishǐ ba。

Qiáozhì：Wǒmen xiān bǎ zìjǐ de shū shōushi hǎo, nǐ cā zhuōzi, wǒ sǎodì, bǎ yào xǐ de yīfu fàng zài yìqǐ。Shōushi wán wūzi, wǒmen yìqǐ qù xǐ yīfu。

（2）

Cóng bān jìnlai de nàtiān qǐ, Dàwèi hé tā de tóngwū Qiáozhì cónglái méiyǒu shōushi guò tāmen de sùshè。Zhuōzi shàng fàng mǎn le shū。Yīfu、xié hé wàzi rēng de mǎndì dōu shì。Jīntiān Dàwèi hé Qiáozhì juédìng yìqǐ shōushi wūzi。Tāmen xiān bǎ shū fàng huí shūjià shàng qù, zài bǎ yīfu cóng dìshàng jiǎn qǐlai, bǎ gānjìng de fàng jìn yīguì lǐ, bǎ zāng de fàng zài yìqǐ, zhǔnbèi qù xǐ。Tāmen hěn kuài jiù bǎ fángjiān shōushi gānjìng le。

28.3 词语（Vocabulary）

1. 乱　　luàn　　adj.　　in disorder, chaotic
2. 地上　dìshàng　n.　　ground

3.	收拾	shōushi	v.	to tidy, to put in order
4.	把	bǎ	prep.	introduces an object to be acted upon
5.	擦	cā	v.	to mop, to wipe
6.	扫地	sǎodì	v.	to sweep the floor
7.	屋子	wūzi	n.	house
8.	从···起	cóng···qǐ	expr. pattern	from (indicating the starting point)
9.	搬	bān	v.	to move
10.	从来	cónglái	adv.	all along
11.	袜子	wàzi	n.	socks
12.	扔	rēng	v.	to throw away, to cast aside
13.	决定	juédìng	v.；n.	to decide; decision
14.	捡	jiǎn	v.	to pick up, to gather
15.	脏	zāng	adj.	dirty, filthy

28.4　注释（Notes）

1. 从···起

"从"是表示时间的名词或短语，"从···起"引入一个过程或时间范围的起点。

This is a device used to introduce the starting point of a process or a scope.

从上个月起，我每天都看中文报纸。（Starting from last month, I have been reading newspapers in Chinese every day.）

从明天起，我要在晚上十一点以前睡觉。（Starting from tomorrow, I will go to bed before 11 o'clock.）

从他到哈佛的那天起，我的同屋每天都早上六点钟起来锻炼身体。（My roommate has been getting up at 6 and exercising for health everyday since the day he came to Harvard.）

2. 衣服、鞋和袜子扔得满地都是

"满地都是"是助词"得"引入的结果补语，表示动词"扔"的结果。"满地都是"的意思是"（屋里的）地上到处都是衣服、鞋、袜子"，有"乱"、"脏"的含义。

满地都是 here is a resultant complement, introduced by 得; it indicates the result of 扔, namely *clothes, shoes and socks were thrown about in such a messy way that they lay everywhere on the floor.*

28.5 语法（Grammar）

1. "把"字结构（The 把-construction）

"把"字结构一般具有下面的形式：

The 把-construction typically takes the following form：

<u>S 把 O V + Complement</u>

从功能上看，"把"字结构用来指明一个对象（宾语）受到主语发出的动作的影响而成为或处于动词补语所表示的情况。例如：

Functionally, it is a pattern used to indicate an object to be acted upon, wherein the subject somehow renders the object into the condition of the complement. The following are some examples：

你应该把黄瓜洗干净。（You should wash the cucumber clean. ）

他把书放到书架上去了。（He put the book on the shelf. ）

我们可以把桌子搬到门口去。（We can move the table to the entrance. ）

你把这些药吃下去，病就会好。（Take these medicine, and your illness will be cured. ）

下面是使用"把"字结构必须注意的地方：

The following should be specially noted with regard to the use of the 把-construction：

A. 这个结构指明一个对象（宾语）加以处置，所以结构中的 O 一般是定指的。例如，上述例子中的"黄瓜"、"书"、"桌子"就是指说话人和听话人都能确定它们所指的定指对象，在英语中这些词前面要加上定冠词"*the*"。

A. Since this structure indicates an object for disposal, the O in the pattern is normally definite in reference. Therefore the 黄瓜，书，and 桌子 in the examples above should be understood as *the cucumber*, *the book*, and *the table*.

B. "把"字结构里面，动词的后面必须有一定的补语表示处置的结果。"＊你应该把黄瓜洗"这样的句子是不合语法的。

B. It is structurally required to have a complement of some sort after the verb in this construction. A sentence like ＊你应该把黄瓜洗 is ungrammatical.

C. "把"字结构整体相当于一个动词短语，所以它的否定形式，是把"不"或"没（没有）"放在整个结构的前面（也就是"把"的前面），而不是只放在动词的前面：

C. The 把-construction as a whole is considered a verb phrase, so when it is negated, 不 or 没 should be placed before the entire construction (namely, before 把) rather than immediately before the verb (V)：

你<u>不</u>可以把自行车放在这儿。(You may not leave your bike here.)

他<u>没有</u>把今天的作业交给老师。(He didn't turn in today's homework to the teacher.)

2. 经历体助词"过"(The particle of experience aspect)

"过"用在动词后面，是表示经历体的助词。句子中使用助词"过"不只是说明这是过去的事情，它也表明与当前状况相关的某种背景方面的信息。

过 is a particle used after a verb to signal experience aspect. A sentence using 过 does not merely narrate a past event. It provides background information that may somehow be relevant to the current situation.

乔治去<u>过</u>上海。(George has been to Shanghai. [Therefore, he knows something about Shanghai.])

我吃<u>过</u>日本菜。(I have had Japanese dishes before. [I can therefore tell you that they are delicious.])

大卫没见<u>过</u>他女朋友的父母。(David has never met his girlfriend's parents. [Therefore he doesn't know what to think about them or whether they would like him.])

我的同屋没有学<u>过</u>汉语。(My roommate has never learned Chinese. [therefore, he doesn't know anything about Chinese.])

有"过"的句子的否定形式，是保留动词后面的"过"并且在动词前面加上否定副词"没"（或"没有"），如上面后两个例句所示。

To negate a 过-sentence, just place the negation adverb 没（or 没有）before the verb but retain 过, as shown in the last two examples.

28.6　翻译（Translation）

Lesson Twenty-Eight　Cleaning up One's Room

(1)

George：Our dorm is so messy, I can't find anything.

David：Yes. Books are all over the floor and the desks, and clothes are everywhere too. If we have some friends over, we won't even have room for them to sit.

George：It is really high time we tidied things up.

David：You said it. Let's do it now.

George：We can each put away our own books first. Then you clean the desks while I sweep the floor. And let's put our dirty clothes together. When we are done with cleaning the room, we can do laundry together.

(2)

Since the day they moved in, David and his roommate George have not cleaned their dorm room. Their desks were covered with books. Their clothes, shoes and socks were all over the floor. David and George decided to tidy up their room together today. They put the books back on the shelves first and then picked up the clothes from the floor. They put the clean ones into the dresser and put the dirty ones together for laundry. It didn't take them long to put their room in order.

第二十九课　谈旅游

29.1　课文（Text）

（1）谈旅游

（乔治和大卫正在讨论他们的旅游计划）

乔治：我的中国地图是不是被你拿走了？
大卫：我没有拿。你找地图干什么？

乔治：二月一号就放假了，看看到什么地方去旅行。你有什么计划？我们一
　　　起去上海吧。

大卫：上海我已经去过了。我打算假期去云南旅游。

乔治：去云南？这个主意不错。那么，我们就去云南吧。

大卫：行。我们坐火车去，怎么样？

乔治：坐火车没有坐飞机快。

大卫：可是坐飞机没有坐火车有意思。

乔治：为什么？

大卫：在火车上，用汉语聊天的机会可多了。

乔治：好吧，我们坐火车去，坐飞机回来，怎么样？

大卫：很好。我马上就去打电话订火车票和飞机票，你去订旅馆，怎么样？

乔治：行！

（乔治打电话订房间）

旅馆：云南饭店，您好。

乔治：我是从北京打来的电话。要订一个房间。

旅馆：什么时候到？

乔治：二月四号。

旅馆：打算住几天？

乔治：一个星期。请问一天多少钱？

旅馆：请问几个人住？

乔治：两个人。

旅馆：双人间，一天一百八十。

（2）坐火车在中国旅游

　　我很喜欢在中国旅游。我更喜欢坐火车在中国旅游。坐上几个小时或者十几个小时的火车，可以遇到很多人。有的去出差或者开会，有的去做买卖，有的回家看自己的亲人，也有的跟我一样去旅游。这些人的工作不同，经历不同，跟他们谈话很有意思，也可以学到很多在课本上学不到的东西。另外，中国地方很大，人们说话的口音也很不一样，跟他们聊天儿不但让我学到了很多东西，了解了中国，而且也提高了我的听力。虽然很多人都说旅游可以看看中国的山水和名胜古迹，了解中国的文化和历史，但是我觉得在中国旅游更重要的是了解中国的

现在。我认为坐火车在中国旅游是一个了解中国的最好方法。

29.2　拼音（Pinyin）

（1）

Qiáozhì：Wǒ de zhōngguó dìtú shìbúshì bèi nǐ ná zǒu le?

Dàwèi：Wǒ méiyǒu ná。nǐ zhǎo dìtú gàn shénme?

Qiáozhì：Èryuè yí hào jiù fàngjià le，kànkan dào shénme dìfang qù lǚxíng。Nǐ yǒu shénme jìhuà? Wǒmen yìqǐ qù Shànghǎi ba。

Dàwèi：Shànghǎi wǒ yǐjīng qù guò le。Wǒ dǎsuàn jiàqī qù Yúnnán lǚyóu。

Qiáozhì：Qù Yúnnán? Zhè ge zhǔyi búcuò。Nàme，wǒmen jiù qù Yúnnán ba。

Dàwèi：Xíng。Wǒmen zuò huǒchē qù，zěnmeyàng?

Qiáozhì：Zuò huǒchē méiyǒu zuò fēijī kuài。

Dàwèi：Kěshì zuò fēijī méiyǒu zuò huǒchē yǒu yìsi。

Qiáozhì：Wèishénme?

Dàwèi：Zài huǒchē shàng，yòng Hànyǔ liáotiān de jīhuì kě duō le。

Qiáozhì：Hǎo ba，wǒmen zuò huǒchē qù，zuò fēijī huílai，zěnmeyàng?

Dàwèi：Hěn hǎo。Wǒ mǎshàng jiù qù dǎ diànhuà dìng huǒchēpiào hé fēijīpiào，nǐ qù dìng lǚguǎn，zěnmeyàng?

Qiáozhì：Xíng!

lǚguǎn：Yúnnán fàndiàn，nín hǎo。

Qiáozhì：Wǒ shì cóng Běijīng dǎ lái de diànhuà。Yào dìng yí ge fángjiān。

lǚguǎn：Shénme shíhou dào?

Qiáozhì：Èryuè sì hào。

lǚguǎn：Dǎsuàn zhù jǐ tiān?

Qiáozhì：Yí ge xīngqī。Qǐngwèn yì tiān duōshǎo qián?

lǚguǎn：Qǐngwèn jǐ ge rén zhù?

Qiáozhì：Liǎng ge rén。

lǚguǎn：Shuāngrénjiān，yì tiān yì bǎi bāshí。

（2）

Wǒ hěn xǐhuan zài Zhōngguó lǚyóu。Wǒ gèng xǐhuan zuò huǒchē zài Zhōngguó lǚyóu。Zuò shàng jǐ ge xiǎoshí huòzhě shí jǐ ge xiǎoshí de huǒchē, kěyǐ yùdào hěn duō rén。Yǒude qù chūchāi huòzhě kāihuì, yǒude qù zuò mǎimai, yǒude huíjiā kàn zìjǐ de qīnrén, yě yǒude gēn wǒ yíyàng qù lǚyóu。Zhèxiē rén de gōngzuò bù tóng, jīnglì bù tóng, gēn tāmen tánhuà hěn yǒu yìsi, yě kěyǐ xué dào hěn duō zài kèběn shàng xué bú dào de dōngxi。Lìngwài, Zhōngguó dìfang hěn dà, rénmen shuōhuà de kǒuyīn yě hěn bù yíyàng, gēn tāmen liáotiānr búdàn ràng wǒ xué dào le hěn duō dōngxi, liǎojiě le Zhōngguó, érqiě yě tígāo le wǒ de tīnglì。Suīrán hěn duō rén dōu shuō lǚyóu kěyǐ kànkan Zhōngguó de shānshuǐ hé míngshènggǔjì, liǎojiě Zhōngguó de wénhuà hé lìshǐ, dànshì wǒ juéde zài Zhōngguó lǚyóu gèng zhòngyào de shì liǎojiě Zhōngguó de xiànzài。Wǒ rènwéi zuò huǒchē zài Zhōngguó lǚyóu shì yí ge liǎojiě Zhōngguó de zuì hǎo fāngfǎ。

29.3 词语（Vocabulary）

1. 地图　　　dìtú　　　　n.　　　map, atlas
2. 被　　　　bèi　　　　prep.　　introduces the agent in a passive sentence
3. 拿走　　　ná zǒu　　　v. p.　　to take away
4. 放假　　　fàngjià　　　v.　　　to have a holiday or a vacation
5. 旅行　　　lǚxíng　　　v.；n.　　to travel; trip
6. 计划　　　jìhuà　　　n.；v.　　plan; to plan
7. 打算　　　dǎsuàn　　　v.　　　to intend, to plan
8. 假期　　　jiàqī　　　n.　　　vacation
9. 主意　　　zhǔyi　　　n.　　　idea
10. 那么　　　nàme　　　conj.　　then, in that case
11. 机会　　　jīhuì　　　n.　　　opportunity, chance
12. 饭店　　　fàndiàn　　　n.　　　restaurant, hotel
13. 双人间　　shuāngrénjiān　n.　　double room
14. 更　　　　gèng　　　adv.　　even, more, further
15. 遇到　　　yùdao　　　v.　　　to encounter, to run into
16. 开会　　　kāihuì　　　v.　　　to attend or hold a meeting
17. 做买卖　　zuòmǎimai　v.　　to do business
18. 经历　　　jīnglì　　　n.；v.　　experience; to experience
19. 另外　　　lìngwài　　　adv.　　in addition, besides

20.	口音	kǒuyīn	n.	accent
21.	听力	tīnglì	n.	aural comprehension, sense of sound
22.	山水	shānshuǐ	n.	landscape
23.	名胜古迹	míngshènggǔjì	n.	well-known scenic spots and historical sites
24.	或者	huòzhě	conj.	or

29.4 注释（Notes）

1. 那么我们去云南吧

"那么"是连词，用来表示顺着前面说的内容而得出结论，与英语的"*in that case*"、"*then*"相似。

那么 is a connective device used to continue what was mentioned previously in the same tone, similar to *in that case* or *then* in English.

2. 机会可多了

"可"是语气副词，用在形容词前面强调形容词所指的性质、属性的程度高。句子里使用"可"时，句子一般用语气词"了"结尾。例如：

可 can be used before an adjective to emphasize its extent or intensity. Normally 了 is used at the end of such a sentence. For example：

他们对我可好了。(They were really very nice to me.)

现在订飞机票可方便了，在电脑上就可以订。(It is really very convenient to book plane tickets now. You can do it on the computer.)

台北的夏天可热了，气温常常在三十五度以上。(Summer in Taipei is really very hot. The temperature is often above 35 degrees Celsius.)

3. 坐上几个小时火车

"上"做补语表示动词所指动作行为的实现或达到预期结果。后面有数词时，表示达到或预期达到的数量。

上 can be used after a verb and before a number to indicate an amount or extent reached or to be reached.

我真想能在北京多住上几天。(I really hoped I could stay in Beijing for a few more days.)

因为要考试，大卫上个星期每天只能睡上四五个小时的觉。(Because of exams, David could only manage to sleep for four to five hours every day last week.)

我到火车站的时候，她的火车快要开了，所以我没能跟她说上几句话。(When I arrived at the train station, her train was about to leave. Therefore, I was only able to say a couple of sentences to her.)

4. 出差或者开会

"或者"把两个可能的事项或事件并列供人选择。虽说"或者"和"还是"都可以译为英语的"*or*"，但是它们在意思和用法上有所不同。"还是"对应于英语"*whether... or...*"中的"*or*"，用在疑问的句子里，请听话人加以选择；而"或者"一般用在陈述句里，对应于英语"*either... or...*"中的"*or*"。使用"还是"时，要求听话人接受两项中的一项而拒绝另外一项，使用"或者"时，听话人可以接受两项中的任何一项。例如：

或者 is used in a statement between two possible entities or events to mean *or*. While both 还是 and 或者 can be translated as *or* in English, they differ both in meaning and usage. 还是, comparable to *whether... or...* in English, is used in a question, explicit or embedded, to ask the listener to make a choice. 或者, on the other hand, equivalent to *either.. or...* in English, is normally used in a declarative sentence to list two alternative possibilities. 还是 requires the listener to pick one against another, whereas 或者 indicates either of the two elements is possible or acceptable. For example：

她星期六来还是星期天来？(Is she coming on Saturday or on Sunday?)

她星期六或者星期天会来看你。(She will come to see you on Saturday or Sunday.)

她星期六晚上常常听音乐或者看电视。(She always listens to music or watches TV on Saturday evening.)

5. 让我学到了很多东西

"让"在这里的意思是"使得"、"致使"，表示前面的事情引起或造成后面的结果：

让 can be used to mean *make* in addition to *let* and *allow*：

这儿的秋天很好看，让我很想家。 （The autumn here is very beautiful. It makes me homesick.）

他说话的样子让我想起他爸爸。（The way he talks makes me think of his father.）

29.5 语法（Grammar）

1. "被" 字句（The 被-sentence）

"被" 字句是汉语的有明确标志的被动语态（*the passive voice*）的句子。"被" 字句典型的句型是：

The 被-sentence is a pattern that explicitly marks the passive voice in Chinese. The typical pattern of 被-sentence is：

N 被 Actor V + Complement

这一句型中，主动者（Actor）发出的动作（V）使被动者（N）处于补语所表示的状况之中。下面是另外一些例子：

In the pattern, N is acted upon by the Actor to result in a situation expressed by Complement. The following are some examples：

我的字典被朋友借走了。（My dictionary has been borrowed by a friend.）
门被风刮坏了。（The door has been broken by the wind.）
鞋子和袜子被扔得满地都是。（Shoes and socks were thrown all over the floor.）
旅馆的房间被订完了。（The rooms in that hotel have been booked up.）

下面是使用"被"字句应该注意的问题：
1）像"把"字句一样，这种句型里动词后面一般要有某种形式的补语。
2）在主动者不便说出或者不能说出时，"被"后面主动者可以省略掉，如同上述最后一例。
3）从历史上看，"被"字句原来只用来表示对被动者来说不如意的事情（例如，主动者的动作使被动者受到伤害或损失）。现在虽说"被"字句的使用已经没有这样的限制，可是在不少情况下"被"字句可能仍然带有这样的意味。

The following should be noted when using this pattern：

1）Like the 把-construction, V in this pattern has to be followed by a Complement of some kind.

2）In cases when it is inconvenient to specify the Actor, or when the Actor is unknown, it can be omitted structurally, as shown in the last two examples above.

3）The 被-sentence was historically used to express an adverse event（i. e. implying that some damage or loss has been inflicted upon the Actor）. Today it is no longer restricted to this use, but it still carries that connotation in most cases.

2. 更（even more）

"更"用于对两项进行对比并指明选中的一项。这种用法的"更"，与其说是表示一种偏好，不如说是表示所喜好的两项间的先后顺序。通过下面两个句子意思的比较，可以看出"更"的作用：

更 is used to show priority rather than preference. This is clear in the contrast between the following two sentences：

（1）我不喜欢喝啤酒，我喜欢喝可乐。（I don't like to drink beer. I like to drink Coke. ）

（2）我喜欢喝啤酒，但是更喜欢喝可乐。（I like to drink beer, but I like to drink Coke even more. ）

句子（1）表明喜欢可乐（*Coke*）不喜欢啤酒（*beer*），而句子（2）表明对可乐和啤酒都喜欢，但是对可乐的喜好排在对啤酒喜好的前面。

While sentence（1）shows a preference for *Coke* over *beer*, sentence（2）implies that, while both are liked, *Coke* comes before *beer*.

29.6　翻译（Translation）

Lesson Twenty-Nine　Traveling

（1）Travel

（David and George are discussing their travel plans）

George: Did you take my China map?

David: No. I didn't. Why are you looking for a map?

George: The semester is over on February 1st. I am trying to find out if I should take a trip somewhere. Do you have any plans? How about we go to Shanghai together?

David: I have been to Shanghai already. I am thinking about taking a trip to Yunnan during the break.

George: Yunnan? That is a good idea. Well, we can go to Yunnan then.

David: OK. We can go by train. What do you think?

George: It is faster to fly though.

David: But flying is not as much fun as taking the train.

George: How so?

David: You would have a lot of opportunity to chat with people in Chinese on a train.

George: That's right. How about we get there by train and come back by air?

David: That's good. I will call right away to make reservations for the train and plane tickets. And you can make the hotel reservations. Is that OK?

George: OK!

(George is on the phone making a hotel reservation.)

Hotel: Hi. This is the Yunnan Hotel.

George: This is a call from Beijing. I'd like to reserve a room.

Hotel: When are you going to be here?

George: February 4th.

Hotel: How long are you going to stay?

George: One week. Can you please tell me how much it is for one day?

Hotel: For how many people?

George: Two.

Hotel: One hundred eighty kuai per day for a double room.

(2) Travel in China by Train

I love to travel in China. Traveling in China by train is even better for me. You meet a lot of people if the ride takes a few or a dozen hours. All kinds of people take the train: people on business trips or on their way to a conference, people who carry their goods to sell elsewhere, people who are going to see their loves ones, and also people like me who are just traveling for pleasure. They are interesting to chat with because they all have different jobs and different experiences. You can learn a great deal from them that you can't from textbooks. Moreover, since China is huge and people speak Chinese with different accents, talking with those people has not only helped me learn a lot and understand China better, it has also improved my listening comprehension. Many people say that traveling in China allows you to see and appreciate the scenery and the famous historic sites, and to better understand Chinese culture and history. but to me what is even more important is that you can learn more about China's present through traveling in the country. I think travel in China by train is the best way to learn about the country.

第三十课 谈印象

30.1 课文（Text）

（1）谈谈对中国的印象

小王：大卫，最近怎么样？

大卫：挺好的，我已经适应这里的生活了。刚来中国的时候，我对一切都很不习惯。

小王：是吗？

大卫：是的。公园里锻炼身体的人这么多，公共汽车和地铁这么挤，这些都跟美国很不一样。

小王：中国的青年人怎么样？

大卫：我认识的青年人不多，都是学生，他们学习很努力，对国家政治、社会问题非常关心。跟美国青年人一样，他们也喜欢听流行音乐，穿牛仔裤。

小王：给你印象最深的是什么？

大卫：给我印象最深的就是中国因特网发展得很快，也发展得很好。很多人在家里就可以上网，我们在学校就更方便了。我常常给我在美国的朋友和家人发电子邮件。

(2)

　　来中国以前，我就知道中国是一个古老的国家，有悠久的历史和文化。我以为古老的国家，一定也很落后。来到中国以后我才发现中国一点儿都不落后，特别是我去过的那些大城市。最近几年中国的经济发展又快又好，人们的生活水平也提高了很多。在很多方面跟发达国家没有什么不同。发展和进步当然是好事，但是交通拥挤、环境污染也是新问题。

30.2　拼音（Pinyin）

(1)

Xiǎo Wáng：Dàwèi, zuìjìn zěnmeyàng？

Dàwèi：Tǐng hǎo de, wǒ yǐjīng shìyìng zhèlǐ de shēnghuó le。Gāng lái Zhōngguó de shíhou, wǒ duì yíqiè dōu hěn bù xíguàn。

Xiǎo Wáng：Shì ma？

Dàwèi：Shì de。Gōngyuán lǐ duànliàn shēntǐ de rén zhème duō, gōnggòng qìchē hé dìtiě zhème jǐ, zhèxiē dōu gēn Měiguó hěn bù yíyàng。

Xiǎo Wáng：Zhōngguó de qīngniánrén zěnmeyàng？

Dàwèi：Wǒ rènshí de qīngniánrén bù duō, dōu shì xuéshēng, tāmen xuéxí hěn nǔlì, duì guójiā zhèngzhì、shèhuì wèntí fēicháng guānxīn。Gēn Měiguó qīngniánrén yíyàng, tāmen yě xǐhuan tīng liúxíng yīnyuè, chuān niúzǎikù。

Xiǎo Wáng：Gěi nǐ yìnxiàng zuì shēn de shì shénme？

Dàwèi：Gěi wǒ yìnxiàng zuì shēn de jiù shì Zhōngguó Yīntèwǎng fāzhǎn de hěn kuài, yě fāzhǎn de hěn hǎo。Hěn duō rén zài jiālǐ jiù kěyǐ shàngwǎng, wǒmen zài xuéxiào jiù gèng fāngbiàn le。Wǒ chángcháng gěi wǒ zài

Měiguó de péngyou hé jiārén fā diànzǐ yóujiàn。

（2）

　　Lái Zhōngguó yǐqián，wǒ jiù zhīdào Zhōngguó shì yí gè gǔlǎo de guójiā，yǒu yōujiǔ de lìshǐ hé wénhuà。Wǒ yǐwéi gǔlǎo de guójiā，yídìng yě hěn luòhòu。Láidào Zhōngguó yǐhòu wǒ cái fāxiàn Zhōngguó yì diǎnr dōu bú luòhòu，tèbié shì wǒ qù guo de nàxiē dà chéngshì。Zuìjìn jǐ nián Zhōngguó de jīngjì fāzhǎn yòu kuài yòu hǎo，rénmen de shēnghuó shuǐpíng yě tígāo le hěn duō。Zài hěn duō fāngmiàn gēn fādá guójiā méiyǒu shénme bùtóng。Fāzhǎn hé jìnbù dāngrán shì hǎoshì，dànshì jiāotōng yōngjǐ、huánjìng wūrǎn yě shì xīn wèntí。

30.3　词语（Vocabulary）

1. 印象	yìnxiàng	n.	impression
2. 挺	tǐng	adv.	very, quite
3. 适应	shìyìng	v.	to adapt, to acclimatize
4. 一切	yíqiè	n.	everything, all
5. 挤	jǐ	adj.	crowded
6. 青年人	qīngniánrén	n.	young people, youth
7. 努力	nǔlì	adj.	to endeavor, to try hard
8. 国家	guójiā	n.	country, nation
9. 政治	zhèngzhì	n.	politics
10. 社会	shèhuì	n.	society
11. 关心	guānxīn	v.	to care, to be concerned
12. 流行音乐	liúxíng yīnyuè	n. p.	pop music
13. 穿	chuān	v.	to wear
14. 牛仔裤	niúzǎikù	n.	jean
15. 因特网	Yīntèwǎng	proper noun	Internet
16. 发展	fāzhǎn	v.	to develop
17. 上网	shàngwǎng	v.	to get on line
18. 发	fā	v.	to send out
19. 古老	gǔlǎo	adj.	ancient, age-old
20. 悠久	yōujiǔ	adj.	age-old, long

21. 落后	luòhòu	adj.	backward; less developed
22. 城市	chéngshì	n.	city
23. 方面	fāngmiàn	n.	aspect
24. 发达国家	fādá guójiā	n.	developed country
25. 不同	bùtóng	adj.	different
26. 进步	jìnbù	adj.	improvement; advancement
27. 拥挤	yōngjǐ	adj.	crowded
28. 环境	huánjìng	n.	environment
29. 污染	wūrǎn	n.; v.	pollution; to pollute

30.4 注释 (Notes)

1. 在家就可以上网

"就"对"在家可以上网"加以强调，这里有非常方便的含义。

就 can be used to mean *as soon as*, *as close as*, and *as easy as*. Here it is used to emphasize the convenience of *getting online at home*.

2. 在很多方面

"在…方面"，用来修饰动词性短语或者名词性短语，指明它们有效的范围。"在…方面"可以译成英语的"*in…respect*"、"*in…aspect*"或"*in…area*"。例如：

在…方面 can be translated as *in…respect/aspect/area*; it is used to modify either a verb phrase or a noun phrase. The following are more examples：

在语法方面他没有问题，但是在语音方面他还要努力。(He doesn't have any problem with grammar, but he needs to work harder on his pronunciation.)

这个国家在经济方面发展得很快。(This country has made rapid progress in its economy.)

王先生在中国历史方面的研究很有名。(Mr. Wang's research in Chinese history is well known.)

30.5 语法 (Grammar)

疑问词任指 (Use of question words to indicate indefiniteness or casualness)
疑问词可以用来任指，指代某个范围里的不确定的某些或某个对象：

Question words can be used in the sense of *some* or *any* to signal insignificance or casualness：

那儿有一家饭馆，我们进去吃点什么吧。（There is a restaurant. Let's go and eat something.）

她一个人住很没意思，她想找谁说说话。（She felt lonely living all by herself. She wanted to find somebody to chat with.）

我住在这栋楼的四层，欢迎你哪天有时间来玩儿。（I live on the fourth floor of this building. Please stop by when you have time some day.）

我们去哪儿走走吧。（Let's go somewhere for a walk.）

用来任指的疑问词用在否定句时，表示"不多"、"有限"这样的意思：

When such a question word is used in a negative sentence, it normally means *not too much*：

你说的和他说的没有什么不同。 （Your words were not very different from his.）

他刚开始工作，现在没有多少钱。（He has just started to work, and doesn't have too much money yet.）

她的朋友唱歌唱得不怎么好。（Her friend doesn't sing too well.）

30.6 翻译（Translation）

Lesson Thirty Talking About One's Impression

（1）My Impression of China

Xiao Wang：David, how have you been?

David：Pretty good. I have already gotten used to the life here. When I first got here, I had a hard time with everything here.

Xiao Wang：Really?

David：Yes. There are too many people exercising in the park, and the bus and the subway are too crowded. It is so different from the States.

Xiao Wang：What do you think about the young people in China?

David：I don't know many young people here. Those I know are all students who work hard and are very interested in the political and social issues of the country. And like young people in the U. S. , they also like pop music and jeans.

Xiao Wang: What are you most impressed with though?

David: What is most impressive to me is how fast and how well the Internet is growing in China. Many people can get online at home. And it is even more convenient for those of us at school. I often send email messages to my friends and family in the States.

(2)

Before I came to China, I already knew that China was an old country with a long history and a rich culture. I thought that an old country must be underdeveloped too. But after I got here, I realized that China was not underdeveloped at all, especially if you are talking about the cities I have visited. China's economy has been growing fast and well in the last few years and the people's living standard has improved a lot. In many ways, China is not that different from a developed country. However, although growth and progress are all good and well, they have also brought about new problems like traffic jams and environmental pollution.

第 1 ~ 30 课词语索引

办理	bànlǐ	v.	to deal with, to handle, to process	11
半天	bàntiān	n.	a long time within a day	15
帮	bāng	v.	to help, to assist	23
帮助	bāngzhù	v.	to help	23
包裹	bāoguǒ	n.	parcel, package	17
保	bǎo	v.	to guarantee	15
报告	bàogào	n.	report	14
报名	bàomíng	v.	to sign up	22
报纸	bàozhǐ	n.	newspaper	17
北京	Běijīng	proper noun	Beijing	17
北京人	Běijīngrén	n.	Beijing person	1
北京城	Běijīngchéng	n.	Beijing City; the city of Beijing	20
被	bèi	prep.	introduces the agent in a passive sentence	29
本	běn	m. w.	measure word for bound sheets	6
比	bǐ	prep.	indicates a difference in manner or degree by comparison.	19
比方说	bǐfang shuō	phrase	for example	25
比较	bǐjiào	adv.	comparatively	15
笔画	bǐhuà	n.	strokes	25
必修	bìxiū	adj.	required course	24
毕业	bìyè	v.	to graduate	20
扁豆	biǎndòu	n.	haricot bean	15
便宜	piányi	adj.	cheap	15
表	biǎo	n.	form, document sheet	11
别	bié	adv.	don't	26
别的	biéde	pron.	other, others	6
饼干	bǐnggān	n.	cookie	27
并	bìng	adv.	used before a negative for emphasis	24

病情	bìngqíng	n.	state of an illness	27
不	bù(bú)	adv.	not	3
不错	búcuò	adj.	good (not bad)	14
不但	búdàn	conj.	not only	17
不过	búguò	conj.	however, nevertheless	21
不客气	bú kèqi	idiom. expr.	you're welcome. (Don't be so polite.)	4
不如	bùrú	v.	not as good as, inferior to	23
不是…就是…	búshì…jiùshì…	expr. pattern	either...or...	15
不舒服	bù shūfu	adj. p.	sick; to not feel well	9
不停地	bùtíng de	adv.	non-stop, incessantly	26
不同	bùtóng	adj.	different	30
不行	bùxíng	adj.	not good (Lit. cannot pass)	25
不用	búyòng	adv.	need not	21
部分	bùfen	n.	part	25
擦	cā	v.	to mop, to wipe	28
猜	cāi	v.	to guess	25
才	cái	adv.	not until	8
才	cái	adv.	only	17
菜单	càidān	n.	menu	13
参加	cānjiā	v.	to attend, to participate in	14
厕所	cèsuǒ	n.	restroom	20
层	céng	n.	floor, story	5
查	chá	v.	to check, to look up	17
茶	chá	n.	tea	26
差不多	chàbuduō	adj.	about, nearly	20
长	cháng	adj	long	18
尝	cháng	v.	to taste; to try the taste	26
常常	chángcháng	adv.	often	5
唱歌	chànggē	v.	to sing a song	14

超重	chāozhòng	v.	to overweigh	17
车	chē	n.	vehicle（which moves on wheels）	12
衬衫	chènshān	n.	shirt	15
城市	chéngshì	n.	city	30
乘车	chéngchē	v.	to ride（in a vehicle）	12
吃	chī	v.	to eat	13
吃饭	chīfàn	v.	to have a meal	10
出差	chūchāi	v.	to be on a business trip	20
出去	chūqù	v.	to go out	14
出租汽车	chūzū qìchē	n.	taxi	19
除了…以外	chúle…yǐwài	expr. pattern	except; besides	16
穿	chuān	v.	to wear	30
传真	chuánzhēn	n.	facsimile, fax	17
床	chuáng	n.	bed	5
春天	chūntiān	n	spring	18
词	cí	n.	word	25
次	cì	m. w.	time; measure word for repeatable events	17
从	cóng	prep.	from	23
从…起	cóng…qǐ	expr. pattern	from（indicating the starting point）	28
从来	cónglái	adv.	all along	28
从早到晚	cóngzǎodàowǎn	phrase	from morning until night	20
打电话	dǎ diànhuà	phrase	to make a phone call	4
打开	dǎ kāi	v.	to open	9
打篮球	dǎ lánqiú	v.	to play basketball	22
打球	dǎqiú	v.	to play ball	16
打算	dǎsuàn	v.	to intend, to plan	29
大	dà	adj.	big, large	5
大灯	dàdēng	n.	main light, ceiling light	21
大多数	dàduōshù	n.	most; a large number of; majority	24

大夫	dàifu	n.	doctor（medical）	27
大概	dàgài	adv.	probably, approximately	25
大门	dàmén	n.	front gate；main entrance	4
大卫	Dàwèi	proper noun	David	2
大学	dàxué	n.	university, college	7
大衣	dàyī	n.	overcoat	15
大约	dàyuē	adv.	approximately	26
代	dài	prep.	for	11
带	dài	v.	to bring	20
但是	dànshì	conj.	but, however	9
当然	dāngrán	adv.	of course	14
倒	dǎo	v.	to switch, to transfer	12
到	dào	v.	to arrive	11
到	dào	v.	to go to；to reach, to arrive	12
到	dào	prep	to（used in defining a range）	18
…的时候	…de shíhou		when；at the time of	11
得	de	structure particle	when used after verbs, it serves as a complement to show the outcome or degree of an action	9
德国	Déguó	proper noun	Germany	1
灯泡	dēngpào	n.	light bulb	21
等	děng	v.	to wait	20
等等	děngdeng	particle	and so on, etc.	17
地	de	structural particle	used to link adverbial and head	14
地方	dìfang	n.	place, district	19
地上	dìshàng	n.	ground	28
地铁	dìtiě	n.	subway	20
地图	dìtú	n.	map, atlas	29
地址	dìzhǐ	n.	address	20

弟弟	dìdi	n.	younger brother	7
第	dì	particle	form ordinal numerals	9
点	diǎn	n.	o'clock	10
点	diǎn	v.	to order (in restaurants)	13
电车	diànchē	n.	trolley bus	12
电工	diàngōng	n.	electrician	21
电话	diànhuà	n.	telephone	5
电脑	diànnǎo	n.	computer	17
电视	diànshì	n.	T. V. set	5
电影	diànyǐng	n.	movie	14
电子邮件	diànzǐ yóujiàn	phrase	email	17
丁	Dīng	proper noun	a Chinese surname	2
订	dìng	v.	to book, to reserve, to subscribe	17
定	dìng	v.	to decide	24
东北风	dōngběifēng	n	northeastern wind	18
东西	dōngxi	n.	things	11
东亚	Dōngyà	n.	East Asia	16
冬天	dōngtiān	n	winter	18
动物园	dòngwùyuán	n.	zoo	12
栋	dòng	m. w.	measure word for buildings	3
都	dōu	adv.	all, both	5
都	dōu	adv.	all	17
豆腐	dòufu	n.	tofu; bean curd	13
读	dú	v.	to read	9
读书报告	dúshū bàogào	n.	reading essay, book review	23
堵车	dǔchē	v.	to have a traffic jam	19
肚子	dùzi	n.	abdomen	27
度	dù	n.	degree (temperature)	18
锻炼	duànliàn	v.	to get physical exercise	19
对	duì	adj.	yes, right	7

方法	fāngfǎ	n.	method; ways and means	24
方面	fāngmiàn	n.	aspect	30
房间	fángjiān	n.	room	8
房子	fángzi	n.	house	26
放	fàng	v.	to put	23
放假	fàngjià	v.	to have a holiday or a vacation	29
放进	fàngjìn	v.	to put in	17
飞机	fēijī	n.	airplane	20
飞机场	fēijīchǎng	n.	airport	20
非常	fēicháng	adv	very, extraordinarily	18
费	fèi	n.	fee	11
分	fēn	n.	minute (used to read the time)	10
分钟	fēnzhōng	n.	minute	19
风景	fēngjǐng	n.	scenery, landscape	17
夫人	fūrén	n.	madam, Mrs.	26
服务台	fúwùtái	n.	front desk	21
服务员	fúwùyuán	n.	waiter, waitress	13
父母	fùmǔ	n.	parents	14
附近	fùjìn	n.	(place) nearby	6
盖	gài	v.	to build	26
干	gàn	v.	to do, to work	22
干净	gānjìng	adj.	clean, neat	5
干燥	gānzào	adj	dry	18
赶快	gǎnkuài	adv.	to hurry, to make haste	10
感冒	gǎnmào	v.	to get a cold	27
刚	gāng	adv.	just (a moment ago)	10
刚刚	gānggāng	adv.	just	7
钢笔	gāngbǐ	n.	fountain pen	6
高兴	gāoxìng	adj.	happy, glad	14
哥哥	gēge	n.	elder brother	7
个	ge	m. w.	measure word	6

各人	gè rén	n.	each individual	20
给	gěi	v. ;prep.	to give；to, for	4,11
跟	gēn	conj.	and（used to connect nouns）	6
跟	gēn	v. ; conj.	to follow；do something with	9
跟…开玩笑	gēn…kāi wánxiào	expr. pattern	to kid sb.	23
更	gèng	adv.	even, more, further	29
工具	gōngjù	n.	instrument, tool	21
工商	gōngshāng	n.	industry and commerce	8
工作	gōngzuò	v.	work	7
公共汽车	gōnggòng qìchē	n.	bus	12
公里	gōnglǐ	n.	kilometer	26
公司	gōngsī	n.	company	20
宫保鸡丁	gōngbǎo jīdīng		Kong-pao chicken（stir-fried chicken with hot pepper and peanuts）	13
古老	gǔlǎo	adj.	ancient, age-old	30
故宫	gùgōng	n.	Palace Museum	19
刮风	guāfēng	v	to blow（wind）, windy	18
拐	guǎi	v.	to turn	12
关心	guānxīn	v.	to care, to be concerned	30
管理	guǎnlǐ	n. ; v.	management；manage	8
贵姓	guìxìng	idiom. expr.	（What is your）honorable surname	2
国	guó	n.	country, nation	5
国际	guójì	adj.	international	8
国家	guójiā	n.	country, nation	30
孩子	háizi	n.	children；child	26
还	hái	adv.	an expression for surprise and unexpectedness.	22
还是	háishì	conj.	or	16
韩国	Hánguó	proper noun	Korea	1

汉语	Hànyǔ	n.	Chinese（language）	1
航空信	hángkōngxìn	n.	international airmail	17
好	hǎo	adj.	well；good	2
好	hǎo	adj.	O. K. , all right	9
好	hǎo	adj.	being a complement after verb to indicate the completion of an action	11
好吃	hǎochī	adj.	delicious	13
好处	hǎochu	n.	benefit；advantage	24
好的	hǎo de	int.	ok, all right	19
好好儿	hǎohāor	adv.	well	14
好几	hǎo jǐ		a couple, a few	16
好客	hàokè	v.	hospitable	26
好在	hǎozài	adv.	fortunately	21
号	hào	n.	number	3
号	hào	n.	date（of a month）	10
号码	hàomǎ	n.	number	8
喝	hē	v.	to drink	13
和	hé	conj.	and（used usually to connect nouns）	5
黑	hēi	adj.	black	15
很	hěn	adv.	very	3,9
很少	hěnshǎo	adv	seldom	18
红	hóng	adj.	red	15
后边	hòubiān	n.	behind	3
后面	hòumiàn	n.	back	3
后年	hòunián	n.	the year after next	7
后天	hòutiān	n.	day after tomorrow	7
护照	hùzhào	n.	passport	11
花	huā	v.	to take, to cost（time）	19
花生米	huāshēngmǐ	n.	peanuts	13
花时间	huā shíjiān	phrase	time consuming	25
画画儿	huà huàr	n.	drawing, painting	22

坏了	huài le	adj.	broken, having a problem	21
欢迎	huānyíng	v.	welcome	8
欢迎光临	huānyíng guānglín	phrase	Welcome!	20
还	hái	adv.	in addition	6
还是	háishi	adv.	still, yet	15
环境	huánjìng	n.	environment	30
换	huàn	v.	to change; exchange, replace	4
黄	huáng	adj.	yellow	15
黄瓜	huánggua	n.	cucumber	15, 27
回来	huílái	v.	to come back	4
会	huì	modal verb	will, may	17
会	huì	modal verb	can, to know how to	22
会议室	huìyìshì	n.	conference room, meeting room	22
绘画	huìhuà	n.	paint, painting	22
火车站	huǒchēzhàn	n.	train station	19
或者	huòzhě	conj.	or	29
机会	jīhuì	n.	opportunity, chance	29
鸡	jī	n.	chicken	13
鸡蛋	jīdàn	n.	chicken egg	13
级	jí	n	level	18
极了	jí le		extremely (used after an adj.)	26
急	jí	adj.	impatient, irritated, worrying	26
急诊室	jízhěnshì	n.	emergency ward	27
几	jǐ	inter. pron.	used to form number-related questions	5
几点	jǐ diǎn		what time?	10
几乎	jīhū	adv.	almost	21
挤	jǐ	adj.	crowded	30

计划	jìhuà	n. ; v.	plan; to plan	29
记	jì	v.	to remember	25
记得	jì de	v.	to remember	23
既不…也不…	jìbù…yěbù	expr pattern	neither nor	18
寄信	jìxìn	v.	to send mail	17
加拿大	Jiānádà	proper noun	Canada	1
夹菜	jiācài	v.	to pick up food with chopsticks	26
家	jiā	n.	family	7
家	jiā	m. w.	measure word for restaurants or shops	13
家常菜	jiāchángcài	n.	homemade dishes	26
家家	jiā jiā		every household	21
价钱	jiàqian	n.	price	15
假期	jiàqī	n.	vacation	29
捡	jiǎn	v.	to pick up, to gather	28
见	jiàn	v.	to see; to visit	14
交	jiāo	v.	to turn in, to hand over, to submit	11
交通	jiāotōng	n.	traffic	19
叫	jiào	v.	to be called; to call	2
教	jiāo	v.	teach	1
教室	jiàoshì	n.	classroom	2
接	jiē	v.	to pick (someone) up, to meet	20
节	jié	m. w.	measure word for a class section	16
姐姐	jiějie	n.	elder sister	7
介绍	jièshào	v.	to introduce	20
借	jiè	v.	to borrow	23
今年	jīnnián	n.	this year	7
今天	jīntiān	n.	today	7
斤	jīn	n.	500 grams	15

紧张	jǐnzhāng	adj.	nervous	16
近	jìn	adj.	close	3
进	jìn	v.	to enter	11
进步	jìnbù	adj.	improvement; advancement	30
进入	jìnrù	v.	to enter	24
经济	jīngjì	n.	economy	8
经历	jīnglì	n. ; v.	experience; to experience	29
九	jiǔ	num.	nine	6
旧	jiù	adj.	old, used	21
就	jiù	adv.	as early as	8
就	jiù	adv.	just, exactly	4
就	jiù	adv.	then	19
居留证	jūliúzhèng	n.	residential ID	10
橘子	júzi	n.	orange	15
句	jù	m. w.	measure word for sentences	16
句子	jùzi	n.	sentence	16
决定	juédìng	v. ;n.	to decide; decision	28
觉得	juéde	v.	to feel, to think	9
开灯	kāidēng	v.	to turn on the light	21
开会	kāihuì	v.	to attend or hold a meeting	29
开始	kāishǐ	v.	to start	2
开心	kāixīn	adj.	happy; rejoice	26
开药方	kāi yàofāng	v.	to prescribe medicine	27
看	kàn	v.	to watch	5
看	kàn	v.	to see; to think, to consider	11
看	kàn	v.	to depend on	23
看病	kànbìng	v.	to see a doctor	27
看见	kànjian	v.	to see, to catch sight of	23

看来	kànlái	v.	it seems, it looks	25
看书	kàn shū	v.	to read (books)	2
考	kǎo	v.	to take (exams)	24
考试	kǎoshì	n.	test, exam	16
可乐	kělè	n.	Coke	13
可能	kěnéng	adv.	maybe, probably	16
可是	kěshì	conj.	but	16
可以	kěyǐ	modal verb	can, may, to be permitted	11
客人	kèrén	n.	guest	26
课	kè	n.	lesson, class	9
课文	kèwén	n.	text (language learning materials)	9
肯定	kěndìng	adv.	certainly	21
口	kǒu	m. w. ; n.	measure word for population in a household; mouth	7
口音	kǒuyīn	n.	accent	29
裤子	kùzi	n.	pants	15
块	kuài	n.	name of the basic unit of RMB in tongue	6,12
快	kuài	adj.	fast	9
快要	kuàiyào	adv.	about to, almost	18
筷子	kuàizi	n.	chopsticks	26
困难	kùnnan	adj. ; n.	difficult	24
拉肚子	lā dùzi	v.	to have loose bowels	27
来	lái	v.	come	8
来	lái	v.	to come; to bring; to give (me)	13
蓝	lán	adj.	blue	15
老	lǎo	adj.	old	8
老师	lǎoshī	n.	teacher	1
冷	lěng	adj.	cold.	18

离	lí	prep.	off; away from (distance)	3
里边	lǐbiān	n.	inside	3
里面	lǐmiàn	n.	inside	5
力气	lìqi	n.	strength, energy	27
历史	lìshǐ	n.	history	16
连…也…	lián…yě…	expr. pattern	even	21
练习	liànxí	v.	to practice	14
练习本	liànxíběn	n.	exercise book	6
凉菜	liángcài	adj.	cold dish, appetizer	13
两	liǎng	num.	two (used with measure words)	6
辆	liàng	m. w.	measure word for vehicles	21
量	liáng	v.	to measure	27
聊天儿	liáotiānr	v.	to chat	14
了	le	modal particle	particle, indicating a new situation set	10
了	liǎo	v.	resultant complement	22
了解	liǎojiě	v.	to understand	19
零钱	língqián	n.	change; coins, small bills	27
另外	lìngwài	adv.	in addition, besides	29
流行音乐	liúxíng yīnyuè	n. p.	pop music	30
留学生	liúxuéshēng	n.	foreign student (liúxué: go abroad for study)	10
六	liù	num.	six; sixth	3,6
楼	lóu	n.	building	3
录音	lùyīn	n. ; v.	tape; record	23
路	lù	m. w.	Unit for bus route	12
路	lù	n.	road, street	19
旅馆	lǚguǎn	n.	hotel	20
旅行	lǚxíng	v. ;n.	to travel; trip	29

旅游	lǚyóu	v.	to travel, to tour	22
绿	lǜ	adj.	green	15
乱	luàn	adj.	in disorder, chaotic	28
落后	luòhòu	adj.	backward; less developed	30
妈妈	māma	n.	mother	7
麻烦	máfán	adj.	troublesome	11
麻婆豆腐	mápó dòufu		Mrs. Ma's Tofu (bean curd with spicy sauce)	13
马马虎虎	mǎmahūhū	adj.	careless, inattentive	23
马上	mǎshàng	adv.	immediately, right away	23
玛丽	Mǎlì	proper noun	Mary	2
吗	ma	modal particle	yes/no question marker	1
买	mǎi	v.	buy	6
卖	mài	v.	to sell	15
满	mǎn	adj.	full, filled, packed	26
慢	màn	v.	slow	9
慢慢儿	màn mānr	adv.	slowly	19
忙	máng	v. ; adj.	busy	16
毛笔字	máobǐzì	n.	calligraphy, brush writing	22
毛衣	máoyī	n.	sweater	15
贸易	màoyì	n.	trade	8
帽子	màozi	n.	hat	15
没关系	méi guānxi	idiom. expr.	that's all right.	9
没有	méiyǒu	v.	when used in front of nouns, means do not have; there is not	5
没有	méiyǒu	adv.	did not	9
每天	měi tiān	phrase	everyday	16
美国人	Měiguórén	n.	American (person)	1
妹妹	mèimei	n.	younger sister	7
门	mén	m. w.	measure word for a course	16

门口	ménkǒu	n.	entrance	12
米	mǐ	m. w.	meter	12
米饭	mǐfàn	n.	cooked rice	13
面包	miànbāo	n.	bread	6
灭	miè	v.	to go out (light; fire)	21
名片	míngpiàn	n.	name card	20
名胜古迹	míngshènggǔjì	n.	well-known scenic spots and historical sites	29
名字	míngzi	n.	name; given name	2
明年	míngnián	n.	next year	7
明天	míngtiān	n.	tomorrow	7
明信片	míngxìnpiàn	n.	postcard	17
母亲	mǔqin	n.	mother	26
拿	ná	v.	to pick up, to take	11
拿	ná	v.	to take; to hold	23
拿走	ná zǒu	v. p.	to take away	29
哪	nǎ/něi	dem. pron.	which	4
哪儿	nǎr	inter. pron.	where	2
哪儿	nǎr	inter. pron.	how is it possible...	22
那	nà	dem. pron.	that	3
那边	nèibiān/nàbiān	dem. pron.	there	17
那么	nàme	conj.	then, in that case	29
难	nán	adj.	difficult	10
呢	ne	modal particle	a modal particle of emphatically demonstrative function	1
能	néng	modal verb	to be able to; to be permitted by circumstance	17
你	nǐ	per. pron.	you	1
你的	nǐ de		your	2
你们	nǐmen	person pron.	you (second person plural)	5
年级	niánjí	n.	grade, year (in school)	16

您	nín	per. pron.	you (polite form)	2
牛奶	niúnǎi	n.	milk	27
牛仔裤	niúzǎikù	n.	jean	30
纽约	Niǔyuē	proper noun	New York	17
努力	nǔlì	adj.	to endeavor, to try hard	30
女主人	nǚzhǔren	n.	hostess	26
怕	pà	v.	be afraid of/that	20
盘儿	pánr	n.	plate, dish	13
旁边	pángbiān	n.	beside	3
陪	péi	v.	to accompany	20
朋友	péngyou	n.	friend	5
啤酒	píjiǔ	n.	beer	13
漂亮	piàoliang	adj.	pretty, beautiful	7
票	piào	n.	ticket	12
拼音	pīnyīn	n.	Pinyin; spelling	25
苹果	píngguǒ	n.	apple	15
瓶	píng	m. w.	bottle	13
七	qī	num.	seven	6
奇怪	qíguài	adj.	odd, strange, weird	23
骑	qí	v.	to ride (astride)	12
起来	qǐlái	v.	to get up	14
气温	qìwēn	n	temperature	18
千	qiān	num.	thousand	25
铅笔	qiānbǐ	n.	pencil	6
前边	qiánbiān	n.	in the front	3
前不久	qián bùjiǔ	phrase	not long ago	26
前面	qiánmiàn	n.	front	3
前年	qiánnián	n.	the year before last	7
前天	qiántiān	n.	the day before yesterday	7
钱	qián	n.	money	4
乔治	Qiáozhì	proper noun	George	16
巧克力	qiǎokèlì	n.	chocolate	6
亲身	qīnshēn	adv.	by oneself, personally (experience)	26

亲手	qīnshǒu	adv.	(do/make) personally	26
芹菜	qíncài	n.	celery	15
青年人	qīngniánrén	n.	young people, youth	30
情况	qíngkuàng	n.	situation, condition	19,24
晴天	qíngtiān	n	sunny day	18
请问	qǐngwèn	idiomatic expr.	May I ask, please?	3
秋天	qiūtiān	n	autumn, fall	18
去	qù	v.	to go	2
去年	qùnián	n.	last year	7
全	quán	adj.	all, whole	7
全身	quánshēn	n.	entire body	27
确实	quèshí	adv.	indeed	25
裙子	qúnzi	n.	skirt	15
然后	ránhòu	conj.	then, after that	24
让	ràng	v.	to let, to allow	21
热	rè	adj.	hot	18
热情	rèqíng	adj.	passionate, warm, enthusiastic	21
人	rén	n.	person, people, human	5
人人	rénrén		everyone	17
认识	rènshi	v.	know	8
认为	rènwéi	v.	to consider, to think	24
扔	rēng	v.	to throw away, to cast aside	28
日本	Rìběn	proper noun	Japan	1
日本人	Rìběnrén	n.	Japanese (person)	5
日用品	rìyòngpǐn	n.	(daily) commodity, necessity	15
容易	róngyì	adj.	easy; easily	25
肉丝	ròusī	n.	shredded meat (generally pork)	13
如果	rúguǒ	conj.	if, in case	19
三	sān	num.	three; third	3,6

扫地	sǎodì	v.	to sweep the floor	28
山水	shānshuǐ	n.	landscape	29
上	shàng	v.	to go	10
上	shàng	v.	to get on	12
上边	shàngbiān	n.	above	3
上次	shàngcì	n.	last time	19
上海	Shànghǎi	proper noun	Shanghai	17
上课	shàngkè	v.	to go to class; have class	2
上面	shàngmiàn	n.	above, on top of	20
上网	shàngwǎng	v.	to get on line	30
少数	shǎoshù	adj.	a few; a small number; minority	24
社会	shèhuì	n.	society	30
申请	shēnqǐng	v.	to apply	10
身体	shēntǐ	n.	body; health	19
深	shēn	adj.	deep	24
生	shēng	adj.	raw; uncooked	27
生菜	shēngcài	n.	lettuce	15
生活	shēnghuó	n.	life	19
声调	shēngdiào	n.	tone	25
省	shěng	v.	to save	25
省钱	shěngqián	v.	to save money	19
师傅	shīfu	n.	master worker, a polite form of address to workers	21
十	shí	num.	ten; tenth	6
十一	shíyī	num.	eleven	6
十字路口	shízì lùkǒu	n.	intersection; cross like "十"	12
什么	shénme	inter. pron.	What	2
什么的	shénmede	particle	and so on	15
什么时候	shénme shíhou		when	10
时候	shíhou	n.	time	10
时间	shíjiān	n.	time	14

食品	shípǐn	n.	food	20
事	shì	n.	thing	4
事情	shìqing	n.	thing, matter	16
是	shì	v.	to be	1
是否	shìfǒu	adv.	if; whether	17
适应	shìyìng	v.	to adapt, to acclimatize	30
收到	shōudào	v.	receive	7
收拾	shōushi	v.	to tidy, to put in order	28
收信人	shōuxìnrén	n.	receiver, addressee	17
手续	shǒuxù	n.	procedure	20
售货员	shòuhuòyuán	n.	salesperson	6
书	shū	n.	book	9
书包	shūbāo	n.	schoolbag	23
书店	shūdiàn	n.	bookstore	6
书法	shūfǎ	n.	calligraphy	22
书架	shūjià	n.	bookshelf	5
舒服	shūfu	adj.	comfortable	5
蔬菜	shūcài	n.	vegetable	15
熟	shóu	adj.	ripe; mature	15
数学	shùxué	n.	mathematics	16
双人间	shuāngrénjiān	n.	double room	29
谁	shuí/shéi	inter. pron.	who	2
谁的	shuí/shéi de		whose	7
水果	shuǐguǒ	n.	fruit	15
水平	shuǐpíng	n.	level, standard	11
睡觉	shuìjiào	v.	to sleep	14
说话	shuōhuà	v.	to speak	9
司机	sījī	n.	driver	19
四	sì	num.	Four; fourth	5,6
四季	sìjì	n.	four seasons	18
宿舍	sùshè	n.	dormitory	3
虽然	suīrán	conj.	though; although	11
岁	suì	m. w.	year(s)-old	7

所以	suǒyǐ	conj.	so, therefore, as a result	16
他	tā	per. pron..	he, him	1
她	tā	per. pron.	she, her	1
台湾	Táiwān	proper noun	Taiwan	1
太	tài	adv.	too	9
谈	tán	v.	talk about	5
谈话	tánhuà	v.	to talk	19
汤	tāng	n.	soup	13
趟	tàng	m. w.	measure word for trips	27
桃儿	táor	n.	peach	15
讨论	tǎolùn	v.	to discuss, to talk about	16
特别	tèbié	adv.	specially	25
踢足球	tī zúqiú	v.	to play football	22
提高	tígāo	v.	to improve	11
体会	tǐhuì	v.	to experience; to realize	26
体温	tǐwēn	n.	body temperature	27
天亮	tiānliàng	v.	daybreak	20
天气	tiānqì	n	weather	18
甜	tián	adj.	sweet	15
填	tián	v.	to fill	11
填写	tiánxiě	v.	to fill	11
挑	tiāo	v.	to choose; to select; to pick	15
跳舞	tiàowǔ	v.	to dance	14
贴	tiē	v.	to paste	17
听	tīng	v.	to listen to	23
听力	tīnglì	n.	aural comprehension, sense of sound	29
听说	tīngshuō	v.	heard about	26
挺	tǐng	adv.	very, quite	30
同时	tóngshí	adv.	besides, furthermore	22
同屋	tóngwū	n.	roommate	5
同学	tóngxué	n.	classmate	4

污染	wūrǎn	n.；v.	pollution；to pollute	30
屋子	wūzi	n.	house	28
五	wǔ	num.	five；fifth	6
舞会	wǔhuì	n.	dance ball	22
西瓜	xīguā	n.	water melon	15
西红柿	xīhóngshì	n.	tomato	15
习惯	xíguàn	v.	to be used to	10
洗	xǐ	v.	to wash	27
喜欢	xǐhuan	v.	to like	5
系	xì	n.	department	3
下	xià	adj.	next	10
下	xià	v.	to get off	12
下班	xiàbān	v.	off duty	10
下边	xiàbiān	n.	below	3
下次	xià cì		next time	23
下面	xiàmiàn	n.	below	3
下雪	xiàxuě	v.	to snow	18
下雨	xiàyǔ	v.	to rain	18
夏天	xiàtiān	n.	summer	18
先	xiān	adv.	first；earlier；before	12
先生	xiānshēng	n.	mister, sir	6
现在	xiànzài	n.	now	8
香	xiāng	adj.	smell good；taste good；delicious	13
香港	Xiānggǎng	proper noun	Hong Kong	1
香蕉	xiāngjiāo	n.	banana	15
想	xiǎng	v.	to miss；to think about	10
想	xiǎng	v.	to think	22
小	xiǎo	adj.	small；little	5
小贩	xiǎofàn	n.	vendor	15
小姐	xiǎojiě	n.	miss, young lady	6
小卖部	xiǎomàibù	n.	convenience store	6
小时	xiǎoshí	n.	hour	19

样子	yàngzi	n.	style, appearance	15
药	yào	n.	medicine	27
要	yào	modal verb.	be going to; want to; plan to	4
要	yào	v.	want; need	6
要是	yàoshi/yàoshì	conj.	if, suppose	22
也	yě	adv.	also; 也不: neither	3, 5
页	yè	n.	page	9
一	yī	num.	one; first	6
一…就…	yī…jiù…	expr. pattern	used to link two actions	14
一般	yībān	adv.	in general	15
一笔一画	yìbǐyíhuà	phrase	stroke by stroke	25
一边… 一边…	yìbiān… yìbiān…	expr. pattern	indicates the simultaneity of two actions.	19
一点儿	yìdiǎnr	num. p.	a little bit	9
一定	yídìng	adv.	by all means, surely	22
一共	yígòng	adv.	in total	6
一会儿	yíhuìr	n.	a little while	23
一起	yìqǐ	adv.	together	5
一切	yíqiè	n.	everything, all	30
一下	yíxià	v. m. w.	used after verbs to indicate a sense of trial or short duration	9
一样	yíyàng	adj.	the same	17
一直	yìzhí	adv.	continuously; straight	12
衣服	yīfu	n.	clothes	15
衣柜	yīguì	n.	closet, chest	5
医院	yīyuàn	n.	hospital	27
已经	yǐjīng	adv.	already	15
以后	yǐhòu	n.	after; later	4, 11
以前	yǐqián	n.	time before	8
以上	yǐshàng	n.	above	15
以为	yǐwéi	v.	thought	19

以下	yǐxià	n.	below	15
椅子	yǐzi	n.	chair	5
因特网	Yīntèwǎng	proper noun	Internet	30
因为	yīnwèi	conj.	because	16
银行	yínháng	n.	bank	4
印象	yìnxiàng	n.	impression	30
应该	yīnggāi	modal verb	should	14
英国人	Yīngguórén	n.	British（person）	1
英汉词典	Yīng-Hàn Cídiǎn		English-Chinese Dictionary	14
拥挤	yōngjǐ	adj.	crowded	30
用	yòng	v.	to use	11
悠久	yōujiǔ	adj.	age-old, long	30
邮局	yóujú	n.	post office	17
邮票	yóupiào	n.	stamp	17
邮筒	yóutǒng	n.	mailbox	17
邮政编码	yóuzhèng biānmǎ	phrase	zip code	17
游览	yóulǎn	v.	to go sightseeing	20
有	yǒu	v.	to have	4
有	yǒu	v.	there is；to exist	5
有意思	yǒu yìsi	phrase	interesting	14
有道理	yǒu dàolǐ	phrase	reasonable, right	25
有技术	yǒu jìshù	phrase	skillful, well trained	21
有时候	yǒu shíhou	time p.	sometimes	9
有一点儿	yǒuyìdiǎnr	adv.	a little bit（used in front of adj.）	10
又…又…	yòu…yòu…	expr pattern	not only...but also	18
右	yòu	n.	right（versus left）	12
右边	yòubiān	n.	right side	3
右面	yòumiàn	n.	right	3
鱼香肉丝	yúxiāng ròusī		Shredded pork with hot spices	13
雨伞	yǔsǎn	n.	umbrella	26

预报	yùbào	n	forecast	18
预习	yùxí	v.	to prepare for; to preview	9
遇到	yùdào	v.	to encounter, to run into	29
遇到	yùdào	v.	to meet	19
元	yuán	m. w.	curtailed form of 圆, the basic unit of RMB	11
圆珠笔	yuánzhūbǐ	n.	ball-point pen	11
远	yuǎn	adj.	far	3
约好	yuē hǎo		to arrange; to agree on a time or place (to meet)	26
月	yuè	n.	month	10
越来越	yuèláiyuè	idiom. phrase	even more	27
杂志	zázhì	n.	magazine	17
再	zài	adv.	Indicates that one action takes place after the completion of another	12
再	zài	adv.	again, once more	17
在	zài	v. ; prep.	to exist; a preposition to indicate the place located at	3
在	zài	adv.	indicates an action in progress	22
咱们	zánmen	per. pron.	we (including both the speaker and the addressee)	22
脏	zāng	adj.	dirty, filthy	28
糟糕	zāogāo	adj	awful	18
怎么办	zěnme bàn	v. p.	what can I do?	24
怎么样	zěnmeyàng	inter. pron.	How is it?	9, 15
炸	zhá	v.	to fry; fried	13
窄	zhǎi	adj.	narrow	24
（车）站	（chē）zhàn	n.	station; stop	12
招待	zhāodài	v.	to host	26

找	zhǎo	v.	to look for	4
找	zhǎo	v.	to give change back	15
照片	zhàopiàn	n.	photo	7
这	zhè	dem. pron.	this	3
这儿	zhèr	pron.	here	3
这个	zhèige		this	2
这里	zhèlǐ	n.	here	15
这么	zhème	adv.	so; such	16
这些	zhèxiē	inter. pron.	these	6
这样	zhèyàng	dem. pron.	so, like this, this way	19
真	zhēn	adv.	really; truly	15
真正	zhēnzhèng	adj.	really; indeed	25
正好	zhènghǎo	adv.	exactly, chance to, happen to	15
正在	zhèngzài	adv.	right in the middle of a process	22
证件	zhèngjiàn	n.	identification card or paper	27
政治	zhèngzhì	n.	politics	30
支	zhī	m. w.	measure word for pens	6
知道	zhīdào	v.	to know	4
只有	zhǐyǒu	conj.	only	17
至少	zhìshǎo	adv.	at least	19
中国人	Zhōngguórén	n.	Chinese（people）	1
中文系	zhōngwénxì	n.	department of Chinese language and literature	3
中间	zhōngjiān	n.	in the middle	3
中午	zhōngwǔ	n.	noon	14
中学生	zhōngxuéshēng	n.	middle school student	7
种	zhǒng	m. w.	kind, category	6
重要	zhòngyào	adj.	important	21
周	zhōu	n.	week	11
周末	zhōumò	n.	weekend	14

主食	zhǔshí	n.	staple food	13
主意	zhǔyi	n.	idea	29
住	zhù	v.	live	8
住宿	zhùsù	v.	to stay the night	20
注意	zhùyì	v.	to pay attention to; to be aware of	25
专业	zhuānyè	n.	specialty, major, concentration	16
转阴	zhuǎnyīn	v	to turn darkly cloudy or overcast	18
准备	zhǔnbèi	v.	to prepare	16
桌子	zhuōzi	n.	desk	5
着	zhe	particle	used after a verb to indicate continuation	26
字	zì	n.	Chinese character	9
字典	zìdiǎn	n.	dictionary	6
自己	zìjǐ	n.	oneself	12
自我发展	zìwǒ fāzhǎn	n.	self development	24
自行车	zìxíngchē	n.	bicycle	12
自由市场	zìyóu shìchǎng	n.	free market	15
总是	zǒngshì	adv.	always	27
走	zǒu	v.	to go; to walk	12
最	zuì	adv.	most	18
最好	zuìhǎo	adv.	had better	27
最近	zuìjìn	n.	recent, recently	18
昨天	zuótiān	n.	yesterday	7, 9, 14
左边	zuǒbiān	n.	left side	3
左面	zuǒmiàn	n.	left	3
作业	zuòyè	n.	homework	16
坐	zuò	v.	to take (a car); to sit	12
坐车	zuò chē	phrase	to ride a bus; to ride a car	12
做	zuò	v.	to do	11, 14
做客	zuòkè	v.	to be a guest	26
做买卖	zuò mǎimai	v.	to do business	29

汉字笔顺

几	丿	几							
了	フ	了							
门	丶	冂	门						
专	一	二	专	专					
以	ㄴ	以	以	以					
节	一	艹	艹	节	节				
可	一	二	〒	可	可				
史	丿	口	口	史	史				
句	丿	勹	勹	句	句				
外	丿	夕	夕	列	外				
讨	丶	讠	计	讨	讨				
亚	一	丅	亚	亚	亚	亚			
有	一	ナ	オ	有	有	有			
年	丿	广	仁	仁	年	年			

乔	一	二	千	天	乔	乔				
忙	丶	丷	忄	忙	忙	忙				
论	丶	讠	讠	论	论	论				
每	丿	仁	仁	句	每	每				
这	丶	亠	文	文	文	这	这			
完	丶	宀	宀	宁	宇	完				
究	丶	宀	宀	穴	穷	究				
译	丶	讠	讵	译	译	译				
张	乛	弓	引	弘	张	张				
事	一	一	一	写	写	事	事			
备	丿	夕	久	各	各	备	备			
治	丶	氵	氵	治	治	治	治			
学	丶	丷	丷	学	学	学	学			
试	丶	讠	讠	讠	试	试	试			
研	一	丆	石	石	石	研	研	研		
是	丨	冂	日	日	旦	早	是	是		
选	丿	丿	牛	生	先	先	选	选		
除	阝	阝	阝	阶	阶	除	除			
紧	丨	刂	収	収	坚	坚	紧	紧	紧	

准	丶	冫	冫	汁	汁	汁	作	准	准		
能	厶	幺	台	台	台	育	能	能	能		
翻	一	亠	平	平	平	采	釆	番	番	番	番
	番	翻	翻	翻	翻						

第 17 课

才	一	十	才						
子	了	了	子						
不	一	丆	不	不					
订	丶	讠	订	订					
北	丨	十	扌	北	北				
且	丨	冂	日	且	且				
只	丨	冂	口	只	只				
包	丿	勹	勺	包	包				
边	乛	力	力	边	边				
再	一	丆	币	再	再				
而	一	丆	币	而	而				
达	一	大	大	达	达				
传	丿	亻	仁	传	传				
件	丿	亻	伫	件	件				
会	丿	人	슥	会	会				
杂	丿	九	杂	杂	杂				
次	丶	冫	汐	次	次				
那	刀	彐	那	那	那				
进	一	二	井	进	进	进			

志	一	十	士	产	志	志	志			
否	一	丆	不	不	不	否	否			
邮	丨	冂	日	由	由	邮	邮			
但	丿	亻	佢	们	佢	佢	但			
局	乛	⁊	尸	尸	局	局	局			
纸	乚	纟	纟	纟	纟	纸	纸			
纽	乚	纟	纟	纠	纠	纽	纽			
现	一	二	千	王	玑	玑	现			
码	一	丆	石	石	石	码	码	码		
明	丨	冂	日	日	明	明	明			
京	丶	亠	产	宀	亩	宁	京	京		
空	丶	宀	宀	宀	穴	空	空	空		
政	一	丁	下	正	正	正	政	政		
查	一	十	才	木	木	杏	杳	查		
贴	丨	冂	贝	贝	贝	贴	贴	贴		
重	一	二	千	亩	盲	盲	重	重		
便	丿	亻	仁	佢	佰	佰	便	便		
信	丿	亻	仁	信	信	信	信	信		
都	一	十	土	耂	者	者	者	者	都	

真	一	亠	广	古	亩	直	直	真	真		
样	一	十	才	木	术	样	栏	栏	样		
航	丿	丆	刀	凢	舟	舟	舡	舮	航		
脑	丿	刀	月	月	肜	肜	脓	脑	脑		
海	丶	冫	氵	汋	沅	汇	海	海	海	海	
寄	丶	宀	宀	宀	宆	宆	寄	寄	寄	寄	
超	一	十	土	丰	丰	赴	走	起	起	超	超
景	丨	冂	日	昌	曼	昙	景	昌	景	景	景
筒	丿	𠂉	𠂉	竹	竺	竺	竹	筒	筒	筒	筒
编	乚	纟	纟	纟	纩	纩	纩	纩	绢	编	编
裹	丶	亠	广	亠	亠	亩	亩	車	裏	裏	裹
裹											

第18课

又	フ	又						
也	コ	也	也					
天	一	二	于	天				
云	一	二	云	云				
少	丨	小	小	少				
长	丿	乍	长	长				
风	丿	几	凤	风				
东	一	左	东	东	东			
四	丨	门	四	四	四			
白	丿	亻	白	白	白			
冬	丿	夂	夂	冬	冬			
阴	阝	阝	阴	阴	阴			
级	纟	纟	纟	级	级			
近	一	厂	斤	斤	近	近		
冷	丶	冫	冫	冷	冷	冷		
快	丶	忄	忄	忰	快	快		
雨	一	厂	冂	雨	雨	雨	雨	
转	一	车	车	车	车	转	转	
非	丨	丨	非	非	非	非	非	

刮	一	二	千	手	舌	舌	刮	刮		
季	一	二	千	禾	禾	季	季	季		
春	一	二	三	声	夫	未	春	春	春	
要	一	厂	币	币	西	西	要	要	要	
秋	一	二	千	禾	禾	秋	秋	秋		
很	一	彳	彳	行	行	行	徂	很	很	
度	、	一	广	广	庐	庐	庐	度		
既	一	彐	彐	艮	艮	艮	既	既		
热	一	寸	才	扌	执	执	热	热	热	
夏	一	一	厂	百	百	百	百	夏	夏	
预	一	卫	予	予	予	孖	预	预	预	
雪	一	厂	声	千	雪	雪	雪	雪	雪	雪
常	丶	丷	严	尚	尚	常	常	常	常	常
晴	丨	冂	日	日	旷	旷	晴	晴	晴	晴
最	丨	冂	日	旦	旦	昇	昇	最	最	最
温	丶	冫	氵	沪	沪	沪	沪	温	温	温
糕	丶	丷	半	半	米	米	粩	粩	样	糕
	糕	糕	糕							
糟	丶	丷	半	半	米	籿	籿	糟	糟	糟

	糟	糟	糟	糟								
燥	丶	丷	少	火	火	灯	灯	炉	炉	煇	煇	煇
	煇	焊	燥	燥								

第 19 课

小	丿	小	小						
习	刁	习	习						
车	一	左	左	车					
比	一	上	比	比					
火	丶	⺌	少	火					
至	一	云	云	云	至	至			
交	丶	六	产	交	夯	交			
花	一	十	艹	芐	芢	花	花		
体	丿	亻	仁	什	休	休	体		
汽	丶	氵	氵	汇	汇	汽			
果	丨	冂	甲	旦	旦	果	果		
的	丿	亻	自	白	白	的	的		
话	丶	讠	讧	讦	讦	话	话		
故	一	十	古	古	古	扩	故	故	
钟	丿	仝	牟	钅	钅	钊	钊	钟	
炼	丶	丷	火	灯	炉	炼	炼	炼	
活	丶	氵	氵	汇	汇	汗	活	活	
宫	丶	八	宀	宀	宀	空	宫	宫	
租	一	二	千	禾	禾	利	利	利	租

站	丶	亠	六	立	立	刦	刲	站	站	
谈	丶	讠	订	诊	诊	谈	谈	谈	谈	
通	⁊	⁊	㇇	甬	甬	甬	甬	诵	通	
堵	一	十	土	圵	圵	坊	堵	堵	堵	堵
票	一	一	一	西	西	西	亜	票	票	票
惯	丶	丷	忄	忙	忙	惯	惯	惯	惯	惯
就	丶	亠	宀	六	亩	亨	京	京	斺	就
路	㇗	口	口	呈	早	足	趴	趵	趵	路	路
解	㇒	㇇	宀	角	角	角	解	解	解	解	解
锻	㇒	㇏	𠂉	乍	钅	钅	钎	钎	锴	锴	锻
锻	锻									
慢	丶	丷	忄	忄	忙	忟	忟	慢	慢	慢	慢
慢	慢									

第 20 课

久	ノ	ク	久						
飞	乙	飞	飞						
片	ノ	广	片						
介	ノ	人	介	介					
业	一	二	川	业	业				
司	丁	刁	司	司	司				
出	凵	凵	中	出	出				
场	一	十	土	圴	场	场			
机	一	十	才	木	机	机			
毕	一	上	比	比	比	毕			
光	丨	丷	业	半	光	光			
早	丨	冂	日	日	旦	早			
各	ノ	ク	久	冬	各	各			
多	ノ	ク	夕	多	多	多			
欢	フ	又	攵	对	欢	欢			
址	一	十	土	圵	圵	址	址		
住	ノ	亻	亻	广	住	住	住		
迎	丶	𠃊	𠂊	印	印	迎	迎		
厕	一	厂	厂	厍	厕	厕	厕		

到	一	工	云	至	至	到	到			
所	一	厂	斤	斤	戶	所	所			
怕	丶	忄	忄	忄	忄	怕	怕			
绍	乚	乡	纟	纟	纫	绍	绍			
城	一	土	土	圹	坊	城	城	城		
带	一	十	卅	卅	卅	帯	帯	带		
点	丨	卜	广	占	占	卢	点	点		
临	丨	刂	圵	圵	临	临	临	临		
览	丨	刂	圵	哘	监	监	览	览		
品	丨	口	口	吕	品	品	品	品		
食	丿	人	人	今	今	食	食	食		
亮	丶	亠	亠	亠	亩	亨	亨	亮		
差	丶	丷	兰	兰	羊	差	差	差		
铁	丿	卜	钅	乍	钅	钅	铊	铁	铁	
旅	丶	亠	方	方	扩	旅	旅	旅	旅	
陪	了	阝	阝	阹	阹	陪	陪	陪	陪	
接	一	扌	扌	扩	扩	护	护	接	接	接
晚	丨	刂	日	日	时	时	晗	晗	晚	晚
馆	丿	个	饣	饣	饣	馆	馆	馆	馆	馆

宿	丶	丷	宀	宀	宀	宀	宀	宿	宿	宿		
续	乙	纟	纟	纟	纟	续	续	续	续	续		
等	丿	𥫗	𥫗	𥫗	𥫗	笁	笁	笁	等	等	等	

第 21 课

工	一	丁	工						
大	一	ナ	大						
术	一	十	才	木	术				
灭	一	厂	灭	灭	灭				
旧	丨	刂	刂丨	旧	旧				
电	丨	冂	曰	日	电				
乎	一	丷	丷	平	乎				
用	丿	冂	月	月	用				
务	丿	夂	夂	务	务				
让	丶	讠	让	让	让				
台	厶	厶	台	台	台				
过	一	寸	寸	寸	过	过			
在	一	ナ	𠂇	在	在	在			
师	丨	刂	师	师	师	师			
灯	丶	丷	火	火	灯	灯			
技	一	十	扌	扌	技	技			
坏	一	十	土	坏	坏	坏			
连	一	左	车	车	连	连			
园	丨	冂	冂	园	园	园			

肯	丨	⺊	⺬	止	肯	肯	肯			
具	丨	冂	月	月	且	具	具			
服	丿	刀	月	月	朋	服	服			
泡	丶	冫	氵	汋	泡	泡	泡			
突	丶	宀	宀	穷	空	穷	突	突		
校	一	十	才	木	杧	栌	栌	柼	校	
理	一	二	王	王	珂	玒	珇	理	理	
辆	一	七	左	车	轩	轩	轩	辆	辆	
傅	丿	亻	亻	仁	佴	佰	伸	傅	傅	傅

第 22 课

儿	丿	儿								
毛	一	二	三	毛						
打	一	十	扌	扪	打					
们	丿	亻	们	们	们					
议	丶	讠	议	议	议					
对	𡿨	又	对	对	对					
名	丿	夕	夕	夕	名	名				
兴	丶	丷	丗	兴	兴	兴				
字	丶	宀	宀	宁	字	字				
好	𡿨	女	女	好	好	好				
报	一	十	扌	扣	报	报				
还	一	丆	不	不	不	还				
足	丨	口	口	早	早	足	足			
哎	丨	叩	口	叮	哎	哎	哎			
咱	丨	叩	口	叩	叩	咱	咱	咱		
哪	丨	叩	口	叩	叩	吗	哪	哪		
室	丶	宀	宀	宀	宀	宊	室	室		
绘	𠃊	纟	纟	纟	绘	绘	绘	绘		
班	一	二	干	王	玎	珏	玨	班	班	

爱	一	一	一	一	严	严	严	严	爱		
球	一	二	干	王	玎	玎	玎	球	球		
游	丶	丶	氵	汒	汸	泸	游	游	游	游	
想	一	十	才	木	札	相	相	相	想	想	想
感	一	厂	厂	厂	后	后	咸	咸	咸	感	感	感
舞	ノ	゠	乍	乍	無	無	無	舞	舞	舞	舞
	舞										
趣	丨	十	土	耂	耂	走	走	赵	趄	趄	趋
	趣	趣									
踢	丨	口	口	早	早	足	足	足	足	踢	踢
	踢	踢									
篮	ノ	乇	竹	竹	竺	竺	竺	竺	笁	笁	篮
	篮	篮	篮								

第 23 课

下	一	丁	下								
马	乛	马	马								
开	一	二	于	开							
见	丨	冂	贝	见							
从	丿	人	从	从							
书	乛	乛	书	书							
如	乚	女	女	如	如						
助	丨	冂	月	且	助	助					
听	丨	冂	口	叮	听	听					
告	丿	丶	牛	生	告	告					
玩	一	三	干	王	玗	玩	玩				
奇	一	ナ	大	本	夻	奇	奇				
虎	丨	卜	吐	广	卢	虍	虎				
放	丶	亠	方	方	扩	放	放				
怪	丶	丷	忄	忆	怪	怪	怪				
录	乛	ヨ	ヨ	寻	录	录	录				
帮	一	三	三	丰	邦	邦	帮	帮			
看	一	二	三	手	看	看	看	看			
笑	丿	⺮	⺮	⺮	竺	竺	竺	竺	笑		

借	丿	亻	仁	什	世	借	借	借	借		
拿	丿	人	合	合	合	拿	拿	拿	拿		
读	丶	讠	讠	讠	读	读	读	读	读		
得	丿	彳	彳	得	得	得	得	得	得		
谢	丶	讠	讠	讠	询	询	询	谢	谢	谢	
跟	丨	口	口	足	足	足	跟	跟	跟	跟	跟

第 24 课

入	丿	入								
为	丶	丿	为	为						
认	丶	讠	讥	认						
办	丁	力	办	办						
处	丿	夕	夂	处	处					
写	丶	冖	写	写	写					
必	丿	心	心	必	必					
考	一	十	耂	耂	考	考				
自	丿	丨	自	自	自	自				
并	丶	丷	兰	兰	羊	并				
安	丶	宀	宀	宊	安	安				
困	丨	冂	冃	困	困	困				
我	丿	二	于	手	找	我	我			
作	丿	亻	亻	伫	竹	作	作			
况	丶	冫	沪	沪	沪	况				
法	丶	氵	氵	汇	汁	泮	法	法		
定	丶	宀	宀	宁	宇	宇	定	定		
怎	丿	广	仆	乍	怎	怎	怎	怎		
修	丿	亻	亻	伊	修	修	修	修		

语	丶	讠	讠	讠	语	语	语	语			
窄	丶	丷	宀	空	空	空	窄	窄	窄		
课	丶	讠	讠	讠	课	课	课	课			
难	フ	又	对	对	对	难	难	难			
排	一	寸	扌	扫	扫	排	排	排	排		
深	丶	冫	氵	氵	汇	汇	泙	深	深		
然	丿	夕	夕	夕	夕	然	然	然	然	然	
数	丶	丷	半	半	米	米	娄	娄	数	数	数

第 25 课

千	一	二	千							
什	丿	亻	仁	什						
化	丿	亻	化	化						
分	丿	八	分	分						
文	丶	亠	文	文						
方	丶	亠	方	方						
正	一	丁	下	正	正					
记	丶	讠	记	记	记					
行	丿	彳	彳	行	行					
问	丶	门	门	问	问					
声	一	士	吉	吉	声	声				
间	丶	门	门	间	间	间				
词	丶	讠	讥	讦	词	词				
画	一	丅	亓	亓	画	画	画			
易	丨	冂	日	尸	吊	易	易			
注	丶	冫	氵	汇	汩	汁	注			
实	丶	宀	宀	宍	空	实	实			
拼	一	扌	扌	扩	扩	拼	拼			
省	丿	八	少	少	尖	省	省	省		

音	、	亠	亠	立	产	音	音	音			
说	、	讠	讠	讥	讱	说	说	说			
特	ノ	一	二	牛	牛	牪	牪	特	特		
笔	ノ	一	仁	竹	竺	竺	竺	竺	笔		
部	、	亠	亠	立	立	咅	咅	部	部		
容	、	宀	宀	宏	灾	突	突	容	容		
调	、	讠	讠	讱	调	调	调	调	调		
猜	ノ	犭	犭	犲	犲	猜	猜	猜	猜	猜	
确	一	丆	石	石	石	矿	矿	确	确	确	
道	、	丷	并	产	产	首	首	首	道	道	道
概	一	十	才	木	朾	杙	根	根	梆	概	概
题	一	冂	日	日	旦	早	早	是	是	是	是
	题	题									

第 26 课

人	丿	人							
女	く	女	女						
手	一	三	手						
公	丿	八	公	公					
主	丶	亠	主	主					
母	乚	口	母	母					
地	一	十	土	圤	地				
夹	一	丶	兯	夹	夹				
伞	丿	人	个	伞	伞				
约	乙	纟	纟	约	约				
极	一	十	木	朾	极	极			
里	丨	口	日	甲	里	里			
别	丨	口	另	别	别				
身	丶	丿	勹	身	身	身			
招	一	扌	护	护	招	招			
房	丶	亠	户	户	房	房			
茶	一	十	艹	茶	茶	茶	茶		
尝	丶	丷	学	尝	尝	尝			
待	丿	彳	行	待	待	待	待		

急	ノ	ク	刍	刍	刍	刍	急	急	急		
亲	丶	亠	立	立	亠	辛	辛	亲			
前	丶	丷	丷	丷	前	前	前	前			
客	丶	宀	宀	宀	夂	宎	客	客			
孩	乛	了	子	子	孑	孩	孩	孩			
菜	一	艹	艹	艹	艹	艹	菜	菜	菜	菜	
做	ノ	亻	仁	什	什	估	估	做	做	做	
停	ノ	亻	亻	亻	广	停	停	停	停	停	
着	丶	丷	丷	兰	兰	羊	着	着	着	着	
盖	丶	丷	丷	兰	羊	盖	盖	盖	盖	盖	
摆	一	扌	扌	扌	护	护	押	押	摆	摆	摆
筷	ノ	𥫗	𥫗	𥫗	𥫗	筷	筷	竿	竿	筷	筷
满	丶	氵	氵	汇	汢	汫	满	满	满	满	满

第27课

力	丁	力								
干	一	二	干							
卫	了	ア	卫							
夫	一	二	ㄓ	夫						
牛	ノ	㇒	二	牛						
气	ノ	㇒	气	气						
生	ノ	㇒	二	牛	生					
瓜	一	厂	爪	瓜	瓜					
头	丶	丷	二	头	头					
奶	〈	女	女	奶	奶					
全	ノ	人	仝	今	仝	全				
医	一	厂	匚	三	至	歪	医			
时	丨	冂	日	日	旷	时				
肚	ノ	月	月	月	肚	肚				
证	丶	讠	订	订	证	证				
诊	丶	讠	讠	讼	诊	诊				
拉	一	扌	扌	扩	扩	拉	拉			
按	一	扌	扌	扩	扩	挼	按	按		
药	一	艹	艹	艻	苭	荮	药	药		

冒	丨	冂	冃	冃	冒	冒	冒	冒		
胃	丨	冂	冃	田	田	甲	胃	胃		
饼	丿	𠂊	饣	饣	饣	饣	饼	饼		
总	丶	丷	丷	兰	兰	户	总	总	总	
洗	丶	冫	氵	沪	汇	泮	泮	洗		
院	𠃌	阝	阝	阝	阵	阵	院	院		
钱	丿	𠂉	𠂉	钅	钅	钅	钱	钱	钱	
病	丶	亠	广	广	疒	疒	病	病	病	
疼	丶	亠	广	广	疒	疒	疼	疼	疼	
烧	丶	丷	火	火	灯	烧	烧	烧	烧	
黄	一	艹	艹	苎	昔	芇	黄	黄	黄	黄
情	丶	忄	忄	忄	忄	情	情	情	情	
越	一	十	土	丰	丰	走	走	起	越	越	越
量	丨	冂	曰	昌	昌	昌	昌	量	量	量
零	一	厂	雨	雨	雨	雨	雨	尹	零	零	零
趙	一	十	土	丰	丰	走	起	起	趙	趙	趙
	趙	趙									

第 28 课

上	丨	卜	上							
扔	一	扌	扌	扔	扔					
扫	一	扌	扌	扫	扫	扫				
决	丶	冫	冫	冲	决	决				
收	丨	丩	屮	屸	收	收				
把	一	扌	扌	扣	扣	扣	把			
来	一	丷	双	平	平	来	来			
乱	一	二	千	千	舌	舌	乱			
拾	一	扌	扌	扩	扒	扒	拾	拾		
屋	一	一	尸	尸	居	居	居	屋	屋	
起	一	十	土	耂	丰	走	起	起	起	
捡	一	扌	扌	扒	扒	扒	捡	捡	捡	
脏	丿	刀	月	月	月丶	扩	胪	胪	脏	
袜	丶	冫	衤	衤	衤	衤	衤	袜	袜	
搬	一	扌	扌	扩	扩	扣	拵	捎	捎	搬	搬
擦	一	扌	扌	扩	扩	扩	扩	挃	挓	擦	擦
	搾	擦	擦	擦						

第 29 课

口	丨	冂	口							
山	乚	屮	山							
么	丿	厶	么							
历	一	厂	厉	历						
水	亅	才	水	水						
计	丶	讠	讠	计						
双	乛	又	双	双						
另	丨	冂	口	号	另					
划	一	七	戈	戈	划					
买	乛	乛	乛	三	买	买				
走	一	十	土	丰	丰	赱	走			
更	一	厂	戸	亘	亘	更	更			
饭	丿	𠂊	饣	饣	饣	饭				
者	一	十	土	耂	者	者	者	者		
或	一	一	戸	戸	或	或	或			
卖	一	十	吉	吉	吉	卖	卖			
图	丨	冂	门	图	图	图	图	图		
店	丶	亠	广	广	庐	店	店			
经	乙	乡	纟	约	经	经	经	经		

胜	丿	几	月	月	肝	肝	胖	胜			
迹	丶	亠	广	方	亦	亦	迹	迹			
被	丶	冫	衤	衤	衤	初	初	衸	被	被	
假	丿	亻	伫	伫	俨	俨	假	俨	假	假	
期	一	十	丗	丗	甘	其	其	期	期	期	
遇	丨	口	月	日	禺	禺	禺	禺	遇	遇	
意	丶	亠	产	立	产	音	音	音	意	意	意
算	丿	仁	丠	竹	筦	筦	筲	管	筲	筲	算
	算										

第 30 课

切	一	七	切	切						
心	丶	心	心	心						
古	一	十	古	古						
仔	丿	亻	仔	仔	仔					
印	丿	𠃌	𠂉	𠂉	印					
乐	丿	仁	乐	乐	乐					
市	丶	亠	亠	市	市					
发	𠃌	𠂊	发	发	发					
老	一	十	耂	耂	老	老				
同	丨	冂	冂	同	同	同				
因	丨	冂	円	因	因	因				
网	丨	冂	冈	网	网	网				
后	一	厂	厂	斤	后	后				
关	丶	丷	䒑	关	关	关				
污	丶	丶	氵	汇	汇	污				
步	丨	卜	止	步	步	步	步			
应	丶	亠	广	广	应	应	应			
社	丶	冫	礻	礻	礻	社	社			
努	𡭔	女	女	奴	奴	努	努			

环	一	二	干	王	玎	环	环				
青	一	二	十	主	青	青	青				
拥	一	十	扌	扪	扪	捐	拥				
国	丨	冂	冂	冋	围	国	国				
挺	一	十	扌	扩	拝	托	托	挺			
挤	一	十	扌	扩	扩	护	挊	挤			
面	一	丆	厂	百	而	而	面	面			
适	一	二	千	千	舌	舌	活	适			
染	丶	丶	氵	氿	氿	边	染	染			
穿	丶	八	宀	宀	空	空	穿	穿			
流	丶	丶	氵	汇	汇	泸	泸	济	流		
家	丶	八	宀	宁	宁	穿	家	家	家		
展	㇇	尸	尸	尸	尸	屏	屏	展	展		
悠	丿	亻	亻	伫	伫	攸	攸	悠	悠		
象	丿	刀	刍	刍	刍	夘	身	象	象	象	
落	一	十	艹	艹	艻	艻	莎	莎	菠	落	落
裤	丶	冫	礻	礻	礻	衤	衤	褙	褲	裤	裤
境	一	十	土	圵	扩	圹	培	培	培	培	培
	境										

词语类别略语表 *

名　　称	词语类别	全　　称	说　明
前缀	prefix	prefix	
后缀	suffix	suffix	
名词	n.	noun	
动词	v.	verb	
形容词	adj.	adjective	
数词	num.	numeral	
量词	m. w.	measure word	
动量词	v. m. w.	verb measure word	
代词	pron.	pronoun	
副词	adv.	adverb	
介词	prep.	preposition	
连词	conj.	conjunction	
助词	particle	particle	
叹词	int.	interjection	
拟声词	o. w.	onomatopoetic word	
专名	proper noun	proper noun	
指示代词	dem. pron.	demonstrative pronoun	
疑问代词	inter. pron.	interrogative pronoun	
人称代词	per. pron.	personal pronoun	
语气助词	modal particle	modal particle	
动态助词	aspectual particle	aspectual particle	
结构助词	structural particle	structural particle	
能愿动词	modal verb	modal verb	

续前表

名　称	词语类别	全　称	说　明
时间短语	time p.	time phrase	
处所短语	place p.	place phrase	
形容词短语	adj. p.	adjective phrase	
动词短语	v. p.	verb phrase	
名词短语	n. p.	noun phrase	
介词短语	p. p.	preposition phrase	
数量短语	num. p.	numeral phrase	
成语	idiom	idiom	
惯用语	idiom. phrase	idiomatic phrase	
习惯用语	idiom. expr.	idiomatic expression	
缩略语	abbr.	abbreviation	
句型	s. pattern	sentence pattern	
语型	expr. pattern	expression pattern	

＊ 词语类别及其略语均用小写字母；兼类的各类间用"；"隔开。

图书在版编目（CIP）数据

汉语基础. 第2册/胡明扬，何宝璋主编.
北京：中国人民大学出版社，2007
中国人民大学对外语言文化学院，美国哈佛大学东亚语文系现代汉语部合编教材
ISBN 978-7-300-08132-8

Ⅰ. 汉…
Ⅱ. ①胡…②何…
Ⅲ. 汉语-对外汉语教学-教材
Ⅳ. H195.4

中国版本图书馆 CIP 数据核字（2007）第 071291 号

中国人民大学对外语言文化学院　美国哈佛大学东亚语文系现代汉语部　合编教材

汉语基础·第二册

主编：胡明扬	主编：何宝璋
编写人员：	编写人员：
岑玉珍	陈珮嘉
陈满华	胡文泽
黄南松	李爱民
张卫国	邱妙津
普通话审订：张卫国	英文翻译：贾志杰
	英文审订：Nick Smith

出版发行	中国人民大学出版社		
社　　址	北京中关村大街 31 号	**邮政编码**	100080
电　　话	010－62511242（总编室）	010－62511398（质管部）	
	010－82501766（邮购部）	010－62514148（门市部）	
	010－62515195（发行公司）	010－62515275（盗版举报）	
网　　址	http://www.crup.com.cn		
	http://www.ttrnet.com（人大教研网）		
经　　销	新华书店		
印　　刷	北京市易丰印刷有限责任公司		
规　　格	170mm×228mm　16 开本	**版　　次**	2007 年 5 月第 1 版
印　　张	14.75 插页 1	**印　　次**	2007 年 5 月第 1 次印刷
字　　数	262 000	**定　　价**	29.00 元（本书另配磁带；附赠练习册）